Heart Lake

A Story of Faith and Deliverance

Richard Glenn

TEACH Services, Inc.
PUBLISHING
www.TEACHServices.com • (800) 367-1844

World rights reserved. This book or any portion thereof may not be copied or reproduced in any form or manner whatever, except as provided by law, without the written permission of the publisher, except by a reviewer who may quote brief passages in a review.

The author assumes full responsibility for the accuracy of all facts and quotations as cited in this book. The opinions expressed in this book are the author's personal views and interpretations, and do not necessarily reflect those of the publisher.

This book is provided with the understanding that the publisher is not engaged in giving spiritual, legal, medical, or other professional advice. If authoritative advice is needed, the reader should seek the counsel of a competent professional.

Copyright © 2020 Richard Glenn
Copyright © 2020 TEACH Services, Inc.
ISBN-13: 978-1-4796-1212-3 (Paperback)
ISBN-13: 978-1-4796-1213-0 (ePub)
Library of Congress Control Number: 2020905728

Scripture quotations marked NIV are taken from The Holy Bible, New International Version®, NIV® Copyright ©1973, 1978, 1984, 2011 by Biblica, Inc.® Used by permission. All rights reserved worldwide.

Scripture quotations marked TLB are taken from The Living Bible copyright © 1971 by Tyndale House Foundation. Used by permission of Tyndale House Publishers Inc., Carol Stream, Illinois 60188. All rights reserved.

Scripture quotations marked KJV are taken from the King James Version of the Bible. Public Domain.

www.TEACHServices.com • (800) 367-1844

"I'm not an avid reader. In fact, I don't read books for pleasure at all. But when Richard gave me a copy of his book, I thought I would just read a few pages. I started reading one Friday night and by the end of the next day I had read the entire book with tears in my eyes during the final pages. What a blessing! Thank you very much for sharing from your heart!"
—Dr. Murrell Tull DDS, Georgia

"*Heart Lake* was gifted to me by my father. He told me, 'You won't want to put it down.' True indeed! The author captivates your attention one chapter to the other with his account of one couple's life during end time events and Jesus' second coming. You won't want to put it down."
—Beth Hallock, Friend, Washington State.

"This book is a testament to the author's love and commitment to God's great plan of salvation. It encouraged me to spend time imagining for myself what end times and eternity might look like and how I would feel and react."
—Debbie Dowling, Sabbath School Leader, Tennessee.

"*Heart Lake* is a beautifully written story with a very eye-opening message that has become even more relevant in today's ever-changing world. Rich with geographical and historical details, it will have you taking a closer look at your own physical and spiritual preparedness."
—Danielle Velez, Program Manager, Knox County Imagination Library, Tennessee.

Table of Contents

Acknowledgments 7
Introduction 9
The Call 10
Global Warming 13
Two Books 16
False Alarms and Dead Ends 19
Identified 23
More Questions 26
The Surprise 31
The Plan 34
A Sabbath Rest 37
Escape 42
A New Day 46
The Investigation 49
The Parents 53
The Mountain Lions 56
Nature Provides a Way 59
An Unwelcome Visitor 62
The Move 65
The Birth 70
Is God Still There? 73
The Burial 76
The Answer 80
Sunday Law 83
Saturday Morning 86
A Lead 91
The Search 93
Discovery 96
Interrogation 99
I Need a Lawyer 104
Reunion 107

The Arraignment. 110
Trial – The Prosecution. 114
Trial – The Defense. 123
Trial – The Verdict 128
The Outreach. 132
The Journey. 137
The Final Quest. 145
Deliverance 149

Acknowledgments

I first thank Doris, my wife of sixty-four years and the mother that made our family the joy that it is and for the support, encouragement, and indulgence with my hobby of authorship.

I thank Barbara Evins for patience, as she used her knowledge and skills in the art of writing and editing to guide me to the finished product. She was a real inspiration and pulled no punches in making sure the final product met her very high literary standards.

I thank Debbie Carithers, Danny Googe, and Danielle Velez for taking the time to read the draft and offer comments for improvements.

I appreciate those in my family, Denise, DeAnn, Sara, and Murrell, who also read the draft and offered encouragement and support as well as constructive criticism.

Introduction

Heart Lake is a story of how ordinary people in small towns in Idaho, far away from the turmoil of the more populous centers of the earth, deal with the turmoil of the last days of earth's history. In particular, how they react to the conflict between God's laws and the laws of men, and how it affects their trust in the relationship with their Creator and Savior, Jesus Christ.

The story is not intended to be a complete or detailed account of the last-day events as revealed in the Bible, particularly as found in the books of Daniel, Ezekiel, Matthew, or Revelation. It is more an account of the personal struggles of one couple as their faith in God is tested.

The characters are fictitious, but the locations are real, and the reactions of the characters offer a hint of how those living in the last days might respond to the conflict between obedience to God and to the power of government. It also offers insight as to how other people may react to those who keep the commandments of God and have the faith of Jesus. Perhaps you will find a part of your story in those characters and events.

The author's intent was not to entertain or provide detailed facts and projections but to suggest a wakeup call to those who consider it irrelevant or inconvenient to keep God's commandments and place their trust in Jesus.

Chapter 1
The Call

"So God created mankind in his own image, in the image of God he created them; male and female he created them. God blessed them and said to them, "Be fruitful and increase in number; fill the earth and subdue it"
(Gen. 1: 27–28, NIV).

Sometime in the future.

"Twin Falls County Sheriff's Office, how may I help you?" Samantha Davis listened intently while the caller identified herself and asked to speak to the sheriff. "One moment, and I will connect you." Samantha held the phone to her chest as she yelled into the inner office, "Sherriff Scott, you have a call on line one."

Sheriff Scott yelled back, "Who is it, Sam?"

Sheriff Scott preferred to call Samantha, Sam. She just seemed more like a Sam than a Samantha, always in charge, spoke her mind, but was also kind and caring. He figured her nature stemmed from her parents, who were devout Christians.

"Someone from the book store on Main Street," replied Samantha.

"Did they say what they wanted?"

"No, they just wanted to speak to you."

"Okay, I'll take it, what line was it?"

"Line one."

"Line one!"

Sheriff Scott picked up the phone, punched line one, and spoke authoritatively, "Sheriff Scott, what can I do for you?"

Sheriff Scott listened quietly as the female voice on the other end identified herself as a clerk at the Main Street Book Store and relayed her message.

"Okay, I'll send someone over to get the information and check the story. How late will you be there?" There was a pause as the clerk responded.

"That's fine; someone will be there in an hour."

Sheriff Scott hung up the phone, walked out of his office, and stopped in front of Samantha's desk, and asked, "Where are Tom and Phil?"

The Twin Falls County Sheriff's Office consisted of Chief Scott, the receptionist, Samantha, and three deputies, Phil Johnson, Tom Mason, and Harry Mason, Tom's son, who had joined the force six months ago. Harry was in Boise for six weeks to complete some additional training.

Samantha checked her computer. "Tom is over at the road to Balanced Rock to check out some reports about the condition of the road and decide if we need to temporarily shut it down. Phil, you may remember, is in Filer doing traffic control at a road construction sight."

"Okay!" sighed Sheriff Scott. "I guess I drew the short straw, so I'll go check out the book store information. I'll grab some lunch on the way, see you in a couple hours."

Twin Falls County is located in south-central Idaho and is bordered on the north by the Snake River and on the south by the Idaho/Nevada Line. Twin Falls County owes its existence to the development of an extensive irrigation system installed in 1903 that allowed the parceling of the fertile volcanic ash-laden land into small farms ideal for raising potatoes and other valuable crops. Twin Falls County has an area of 1,928 square miles and a population of approximately 90,000 people, not large or densely populated compared to the rest of the world.

The city of Twin Falls is the largest city in the county and also the county seat. The name "Twin Falls" came from the "twin" falls that gave a spectacular picture of the cascading waters of the Snake River as it made its way through the Snake River Canyon on the course to a rendezvous with the Columbia River and eventually the Pacific Ocean.

Sheriff Darrin Scott graduated from a private school in Caldwell, Idaho, and spent four years in the U. S. Army Military Police Corps. After four years, he decided to return to civilian life and back to his roots in

Twin Falls. He also returned to marry his high school sweetheart, Sherri, who had a daughter from a short, previous marriage. He loved her dearly as well as her daughter, Chelsea, whom he later adopted. Chelsea was an investigative reporter for the Salt Lake Tribune.

In the past, he had driven semi-trucks for a number of companies and then decided that that life was not for him, so he joined the Twin Falls Police Department. After eight years in the Twin Falls Police Department, and with the urging of some friends and the mayor, he decided to run for Twin Falls County Sheriff. Much to his surprise, he won and was reelected several times.

During the twenty-eight years as sheriff, he had seen many changes in law enforcement, particularly in the United States and to some extent in Twin Falls County. His predecessor insisted that "This job has too much bull," and Sheriff Scott agreed with him. He was genuinely concerned about the lack of respect for law enforcement but also the cultural changes that had spread around the world. He was particularly troubled by the recent cultural change that prompted the Main Street Book Store clerk to call his office.

Chapter 2
Global Warming

Sheriff Scott parked his squad car in the lot in front of the Depot Grill. The Depot Grill was so named because it adjoined the old Union Pacific Railroad station that had long since been abandoned for lack of any rail passenger service along the Idaho Short Line that stretched from Murtaugh to Buhl. Freight trains still passed by on a random basis, but all was quiet as he entered the Grill, sat down at his customary table, and nodded to Grace, the waitress. Without a word, she entered his usual order of a hamburger, fries, and a Coke. The Depot Grill served the best burgers in town

His thoughts turned to what was on his mind as he waited for his food. He was still troubled by the recent cultural change that prompted the Main Street Book Store clerk to call his office. He believed in God, the One that created and controlled the universe and was always troubled by any man-made law that conflicted with God's laws. He felt this new law restricting couples from having children was in direct conflict with God's wishes, as expressed in Genesis. All because of the world's fear of global warming.

The actual beginning of the "global warming" debate was not well documented, but some publications indicate that it may have begun in the 1970s. The debate was mostly limited to the academic world until it burst into the public debate with the release of the 2006 documentary, *An Inconvenient Truth*.

"Environmental Believers" (EBs) claimed that the dramatic increase in the carbon dioxide (CO_2) gas in the atmosphere was causing a greenhouse effect that resulted in the rise of the average temperature of the earth. Adding a doom's day element to the theory led to the conclusion that unless the increase in CO_2 in the atmosphere is checked, the polar ice will melt, the oceans will rise, and the inhabited coastal cities and lands of the world will be submerged, wiping out millions of homes and causing catastrophic economic losses. The consensus of proponents of the global warming theory was that the world needed to reduce CO_2 emissions.

The EBs had adopted the global warming cry as a creed, and it had become their religion, with no room for God and His power to control the universe. People were the cause, and people had to do something to control it. God was out of the picture.

Politicians proposed a tax on emissions containing CO_2, especially emissions from coal-fired power plants, but it was never passed by Congress. Regulations requiring increased vehicle fuel economy, however, were enacted by Congress. So the debate continued without a real effort to reach any meaningful control mechanism to curb the emission of greenhouse gases and global warming.

Then a sequel titled *An Inconvenient Sequel, Truth to Power* was released in 2017. People and governments around the world began to take the threat more seriously and focused on the root cause, consumption by humans. No matter how much effort was exerted by governments and interest groups to limit the greenhouse emissions through limiting consumption, the world population continued to increase and consumed more greenhouse gas-emitting energy and products.

The world leaders declared that the world was in crisis. They gathered in Brussels, Belgium, to address the crisis and elected a very charismatic young man from central Europe to be the world leader and gave him the task and the power to come up with a solution to the crisis. He immediately offered the final and logical solution. Limit the population of the earth.

Initially, the world leaders agreed on a massive worldwide advertising and promotional campaign to educate the world population on the dangers of global warming and encouraging the restriction of the number of children in the family to two, low enough to stop the expansion of the population but enough to provide a sufficiently large enough workforce to sustain the world economy.

That did not work because it was largely ignored except for a few avid anti-global warming activists, and it had no incentive attached. Families kept having as many children as they wanted.

The next failed attempt offered a monetary incentive applied to the first two children in a family and a graduated monetary penalty for each child added to the family over two. That worked better, but the population still did not stop increasing.

In desperation the world leaders under the leadership of the elected world leader came up with a simple final solution. Limit the number of worldwide births each year to the optimum necessary to maintain the necessary workforce and limit consumption of greenhouse gas-producing products and services that would reverse the global-warming trend.

They established a permit system. Without a permit couples could not bear children, and if they did, they faced heavy consequences, which included mandatory abortion, subsequent sterilization of both the mother and the father, and a heavy fine and/or imprisonment. If the child had been born without a permit, it was removed from the parents, sterilized, and placed in a government home. The permit system also allowed the world leaders to be selective on who got the permits, giving them control of the quality of children allowed to be born.

This was the change in the world culture that Sheriff Scott objected to the most, for it fell on the local law enforcement officers to help the state and federal agencies to enforce the new policy. He hated his responsibility that could prevent other law-abiding citizens of Twin Falls County from enjoying the blessings and joys of parenthood. He had been lucky so far, however. As far as he knew, there had not been an illegal birth in Twin Falls County since the new policy became the law. In fact, neither had one birth permit been issued in the county during the same period. Twin Falls County Hospital had even shut down the OB section for lack of any births. He also felt strongly that this was just another example where people had to choose whether to obey God's commands or the laws of man.

With a heavy heart and a feeling of dread, he finished his cheeseburger and fries, took one last sip of Diet Coke, left his payment, including a generous tip on the table, exited the Depot Grill, and climbed into his squad car for the slow drive to the Main Street Book Store.

Chapter 3
Two Books

As Sheriff Scott drove from the Main Street Book Store back to the office, he let his mind try to process what he had heard at the book store but was interrupted as he drove into the parking lot by the sheriff's deputy, Tom Mason, exiting his cruiser. Neither spoke as they walked together to the front door and entered.

Sam got up from her chair behind her desk and met them as they entered. "Well, Sheriff, what did you find at the book store?"

Tom was startled as he first looked at Sam and then at the sheriff, wondering what could be more important than his report about the road conditions at Balanced Rock, but he remained silent as Sheriff Scott dropped his heavy frame in the chair in front of Sam's desk.

"It's probably a false alarm and nothing to it. You know Betty! She gets excited sometimes, jumps to conclusions, and sees a problem where there isn't any."

Betty was Betty Johnson, the owner of the Main Street Book Store and self-appointed town busybody.

"When I walked into the book store, she made a beeline for me and exclaimed, "A young man came into the store this morning and bought two books!"

Tom Mason, who had been silent until this moment, could not contain himself and blurted out, "What's wrong with that? That Betty, she sees a ghost in every corner and a conspiracy if the sun comes up."

Sam gave Tom an impatient look. "Tom, let Sheriff Scott finish the story."

Sheriff Scott cleared his throat. "As I told you before, Betty said a young man came into the store this morning and purchased two books."

"What books?" quizzed Sam.

"One was on wilderness living, and the other one was titled, *Survival Guide to Midwifery.*"

"So?" questioned Tom.

"Betty is certain that it has something to do with the regulation against having a baby without a permit," explained Sheriff Scott, "and if that is the case, we may have a problem. We will be expected to investigate, find the young man, and if he has a wife who is pregnant, arrest them, and turn them over to the federal agents from Homeland Security."

Sam and Tom looked at each other, and Sam finally spoke. "Amazing, we have never had anyone go that far in the two years since the regulation became law. Everyone that I know has been very careful to use the best and newest birth control methods and medications. They are readily available at little or no cost, so why would anyone take the chance? The penalty is so severe. Why would you want to put your family and a child at such risk?"

> *We will be expected to investigate, find the young man, and if he has a wife who is pregnant, arrest them, and turn them over to the federal agents from Homeland Security.*

Tom came out of his state of disbelief and asked the logical question, "Sheriff, did Betty know who the young man was or know anything that might lead to his identity?"

"No!" answered the Sheriff, "and there was no security camera that might give us a clue."

"What about a credit card?"

"He paid with cash."

"Well, is it possible we could get a fingerprint from the bills he used to make the purchase?"

"Highly unlikely; the bills got mixed up in the drawer, so we don't know which bills belonged to the young man. Besides, the cash accumulated during the morning was taken to the bank at noon, so that further diluted any chance of knowing which bills are the specific ones."

"Dead end!" muttered Tom.

"Not exactly. Betty gave me a pretty good description that we can translate into a reasonable sketch. We can use that to pass around and post to see if anyone knows who the young man may be. I'll send the sketch artist we use to interview Betty and see if that will give us the sketch we need to find the young man and clear him of any problem. Who knows? Maybe he doesn't even have a wife to get pregnant. Wouldn't that be a twist?"

With that, Tom and the sheriff returned to their offices, and Sam slipped into her chair, each lost in thoughts about how they might proceed to take care of "the problem" in a way that would save the County embarrassment and deal kindly and understandingly with the mystery young man or couple if that turned out to be the case. So far, all they had was speculation and suspicion based on the purchase of two books.

Chapter 4
False Alarms and Dead Ends

It took a couple of days and two interviews with Betty Johnson, but the sketch artist, after many attempts, finally completed the final likeness of the mystery book purchaser. Sheriff Scott had several hundred printed, and he and Tom spent the next two days circulating them. Phil was not able to help because he had to continue traffic control at the road construction site. The sketch was also printed in the Twin Falls paper, and Sheriff Scott even sent one to his step-daughter in Salt Lake City to see if she recognized the man. She did not but promised to pass it around.

The office phone rang, and Sam answered, "Twin Falls County Sheriff. How may I help you?" There was a pause as Sam intently listened to the caller and then wrote down a name and address. She got up from her desk, entered Sheriff Scott's office, and laid the note with the name and address on his desk:

"Mrs. King thinks the mystery man is her next-door neighbor."

Sheriff Scott rose from his desk, nodded at Sam, grabbed the note, and stuck his head in Tom's office. "Tom, we may have a lead on the mystery man; let's go check it out."

Mrs. King and her husband Ray lived on Indian Trail in a small housing development in northeast Twin Falls that was composed of fairly new neat, well-kept, ranch starter homes. They had moved from North Carolina to Twin Falls to be closer to her parents that lived in Salt Lake City and her grandparents that lived in Buhl about sixteen miles west of Twin Falls.

LeAnn King had worked at the Twin Falls County Hospital in the labor and delivery department until the cutback caused by the worldwide population control regulations. She missed working with expectant mothers and helping them through the trauma of delivering a baby. She was the one that had called the sheriff's office even though she didn't know why the sketch she had seen at the Albertson's grocery store was important.

Ray was a CRNA (Certified Registered Nurse Anesthetist) at the Twin Falls Clinic. He considered the reduction in childbirths a blessing. He had fewer calls nights and weekends to assist in delivering the babies. He hated those middle-of-the-night calls.

Sheriff Scott and Tom parked in front of the King house. It had only taken a few minutes to drive from the office to the King home, so they did not have much time to develop a plan for the interview, except that Sheriff Scott suggested that he ask the questions, and Tom take notes.

They walked to the front door and rang the doorbell. It wasn't long before LeAnn King opened the door and inquired, "Yes, how may I help you?"

Sheriff Scott and Tom showed her their badges,

"Mrs. King, I am Sheriff Scott, and this is my deputy Tom Mason. May we come in? We'd like to ask you a few questions."

"Sure," responded LeAnn, "Come in!"

They entered the small house, and LeAnn invited them into the living room. "Won't you have a seat? Can I get you anything? Something to drink?"

As he and Tom took a seat on the couch, the Sheriff responded.

"No thanks, Mrs. King. We're fine, but thanks anyway."

Tom remained silent.

There was a moment of silence as the sheriff produced a copy of the mystery-man sketch, offered it to Mrs. King, and asked, "Mrs. King, we understand from your call to our office that you think you may know the identity of the man in this sketch?"

LeAnn took the sketch, looked at it for a moment, handed it back to Sheriff Scott, and replied. "Yes, I believe it looks a lot like Max Wilkins, our neighbor next door."

"Are you sure?"

"Well, it's not a very good picture, and we don't see him and his wife a lot, but I am reasonably sure. They haven't lived there very long, and my husband might be the best to say because he and the neighbor talk once in a while when they are working in the yard. But my husband won't be home for some time."

Sheriff Scott asked, "Perhaps one of the other neighbors could be of help. We certainly don't want to disturb your next-door neighbor unless we are very sure that he is the man in the sketch."

Somewhat relieved with the possibility of not being involved anymore, LeAnn quickly gave Sheriff Scott the names one of the other neighbors. "Barbara and Mark Wehtje, and they're in the house across the street. I think Barbara is at home!"

"Thank you, Mrs. King," as they got up and headed for the door, "You have been most helpful," assured the sheriff.

Sheriff Scott and Tom crossed the street and approached the front door. After ringing the bell, they heard the sound of a door slamming, footsteps, and a breathless female voice yelled through the door, "Who is it?"

"Twin Falls County Sheriff and deputy Tom Mason, ma'am. May we have a word with you?"

The woman cracked the door just enough to see who it was and asked, "May I see some ID?"

Sheriff Scott and Tom offered their badges. "Are you Barbara Wehtje?"

"Yes, that's me!"

Satisfied, Sheriff Scott pressed ahead. "This will only take a few minutes. We need to ask you a question or two."

Sheriff Scott pulled out the mystery-man sketch and offered it to Barbara through the screen. "Is this a picture of Max Wilkins, your neighbor across the street?"

Barbara opened the door wider and intently studied the sketch. "Definitely not! No, that is not a picture of Mr. Wilkins. Who said it was?"

"Your other neighbor across the street, Mrs. King, She seemed to think it was, and she was pretty sure it was when she called our office."

By that time, Barbara had opened the screen door, stepped out on the porch, taken a closer look at the sketch, and emphatically exclaimed. "LeAnn is a great neighbor and friend, but sometimes she leaps before she looks. I love her to death, almost like a sister, but I am afraid in this case she is wrong. You can ask all the other neighbors in the cul-de-sac, and they will tell you the same thing. That is definitely not a picture of Mr. Wilkins, no way! Sorry!"

Sheriff Scott and Tom turned to go when Barbara asked. "Why are you trying to find the man in the sketch? Has he done something illegal?"

Sheriff Scott evasively replied, "We aren't sure. We are just trying to locate him and ask him some questions about his involvement in an incident last week."

"Well, then, it definitely was not Mr. Wilkins because last week he and his wife were in California on vacation.

"Thank you for your help, ma'am!"

He and Tom returned to their car and drove away in silence. Finally, Tom broke the silence. "What next?"

Sheriff Scott gave a long sigh. "I guess that was a dead-end, so we will just have to be patient and see if we get any other leads."

For the next few days, the office was flooded with calls claiming that they were certain they knew the identity of the person in the sketch. Sheriff Scott and Tom spent hours following up on all the calls without finding the mystery man.

As the days went by, the calls dwindled down and finally stopped. Every lead had been investigated, but the identity of the book purchaser remained a mystery. Sam, Sheriff Scott, and the deputies put locating the mystery book purchaser on the back burner and returned their attention to other more pressing matters.

> *Sheriff Scott and Tom spent hours following up on all the calls without finding the mystery man.*

Chapter 5
Identified

Harry Mason arrived home Friday evening from his special training in Boise and had a restful and happy weekend with his wife and little six-year-old daughter. It was good to be back in Twin Falls, but he was thankful that he had the chance to get the special training. He had always wanted to be a law enforcement officer, as he watched his dad serve many years as a deputy sheriff. He had lived his whole life in Twin Falls, graduated from Twin Falls High School and earned an associate of arts degree in criminal justice from the College of Southern Idaho. He was hired as a deputy sheriff right after completing his degree. He and his wife, Amy, were married shortly after he was hired.

Monday morning, Harry kissed Amy and daughter goodbye and drove to the sheriff's office to report for duty. He had no idea what Sheriff Scott might have in mind for him to do today, but he was sure that whatever it was, it would keep him busy. When he arrived at the office, the other cruisers were already in the parking lot along with Samantha's silver Honda. He walked into the reception room and declared, "I'm back!"

Samantha looked up from her computer and flashed him a smile. "Welcome back! How was Boise?"

He gave her a thumbs-up, winked, and started to answer her when the sheriff, his dad, and Phil piled out of their offices, shook his hand, slapped him on the back, and also gave him a "Welcome back!"

Sheriff Scott invited Harry to join him in his office. They sat on opposite sides of Sheriff Scott's desk, and Harry asked. "What's been happening, anything exciting?"

"Nothing exciting; everything has been very quiet, no major accidents, fires, or crimes since you left, but we did have a wild goose chase a couple weeks ago. We spent a lot of time and manpower trying to find a young man to ask him some questions about two books he bought at the Main Street Book Store, but even after following up on several leads, we drew a blank."

Harry looked bewildered, "What was so important about buying books that you spent all that time and effort trying to locate him?"

Sheriff Scott averted Harry's stare, cleared his throat, and explained, "You remember that a couple years ago it became the law that couples could not legally have children without the proper permit from the Department of Homeland Security, and there were stiff penalties if they did. Well, couples in Twin Falls County took the law very seriously, and we have not had any violations as far as we know. Well, the young man in question bought a book on wilderness living and midwifery, so the owner of the book store got suspicious, notified us, and we tried to find the young man for questioning. We circulated a sketch and followed up many leads but came up empty-handed."

As the sheriff related the story, Harry recalled how thankful he and Amy had been that their daughter was born before the law was passed. He and Amy had talked about wanting another child and had applied for a permit but had about given up hope that they would ever be granted one. Coming back to the issue, he asked Sheriff Scott if he could have a look at the sketch.

Sherriff Scott retrieved a copy of the sketch from his desk and handed it to Harry. Harry looked at it closely for a few minutes and declared, "I think I know this guy. He's from Buhl. He played football, basketball, and baseball for Buhl High School, and I played against him several times. I think his name was Casey, but I don't remember his last name. Did you get any leads from Buhl?"

Sheriff Scott admitted. "No, and we didn't even think about checking there, all the leads came from people here in Twin Falls, and since all of them were false alarms, we gave up and didn't expand the search to the other towns."

"Well, I'm pretty certain that the man in the sketch is Casey, and he lives, or at least he used to live in Buhl. I haven't kept track of him at all, but I do know he played for the Buhl Indians."

"Well, let's check it out," suggested the sheriff.

Chapter 6
More Questions

On the sixteen-mile drive from Twin Falls to Buhl, a town located on the old Oregon Trail in the western half of Twin Falls County, Sheriff Scott and Harry formulated a plan. They decided to first contact the Buhl police and go from there. Upon entering Buhl on US Route 30, they turned northwest on Broadway, drove through the only signal light in the town and arrived at 201 Broadway North, parked, and entered a modern single-story building with a large concrete slab sign that indicated it was the Buhl City Hall.

They were greeted by a friendly, smiling young lady behind a desk with a nameplate indicating that she was Teri McGill, Office Manager.

"May I help you?" she asked.

Sheriff Scott introduced himself and Harry. "We're from the Twin Falls County Sheriff's Department, I am Sheriff Scott, and this is Deputy Harry Mason. We would like to speak to Chief Pryor."

"Chief Pryor is not in the office right now, but maybe Sergeant Hamilton can help you."

She punched the intercom button. "Sergeant Hamilton, the Twin Falls County Sheriff and deputy sheriff Mason would like to talk to you."

Then turning to Sheriff Scott and Harry, she offered them a seat. "Sergeant Hamilton will see you in a moment."

While they waited, Sheriff Scott surveyed the office. Two halls branched off of the reception area, and he could see four offices in each hall. Sergeant Hamilton emerged from one of the rooms and offered his greetings,

"Hi, I'm Jay Hamilton. Welcome to Buhl. Come into my office."

Sheriff Scott and Harry followed him into a small office that contained a government-issue desk and chair, a small bookcase, and two guest chairs in front of the desk. Sergeant Hamilton sat in the desk chair and motioned for them to sit in the two guest chairs.

"What brings you to Buhl?" he asked.

Sheriff Scott explained why they were there and showed him a copy of the sketch that they had circulated in Twin Falls.

Sergeant Hamilton quietly eyed the sketch for a few minutes and finally remarked, "This doesn't look like anyone I know. Do you have a better picture or additional information?"

Harry responded, "I think this is a guy who played for the Buhl Indians football and baseball teams the same time I played for the Twin Falls Bruins teams. If I remember, I think his name was Casey, but I don't remember his last name."

Sergeant Hamilton took another long look at the sketch, cleared his throat, and declared, "By George, I think you're right, that does resemble Casey Denney. He did play for the Indians, and I think he works at Rangen. You'll probably find him there. Would you like me to go with you to see him?"

> *Sergeant Hamilton quietly eyed the sketch for a few minutes and finally remarked, "This doesn't look like anyone I know. Do you have a better picture or additional information?"*

Sheriff Scott rose from his chair, extended his hand, and replied, "Thanks for your help, but I think we can go talk to him. It may be a wild goose chase, so there is no need to waste any more of your time."

Sergeant Hamilton took the sheriff's extended hand and, with a firm handshake, offered, "I understand, and you are certainly welcome in Buhl anytime. That is one thing we like about the law enforcement groups in

Twin Falls County. We help each other out but stay out of the way when necessary. But anytime we can, we are glad to help. Just let me know."

After Sheriff Scott and Harry were back in the squad car, Sheriff Scott suggested. "Harry, Google Rangen, and let's refresh our memory of the company and what they do. It may give us a better understanding of Casey Denney and what are his interests and capabilities."

Harry opened his laptop computer, and after a few minutes, the computer booted up, and he began to read the Rangen company description on their web page. He read,

> "Rangen, Inc. is a diverse agriculture-based business started in 1925 with specialty operations in aquaculture, general feeds, and commodities.
>
> The Aquaculture Division produces and markets specialized high-quality aquaculture feeds for trout, salmon, and shrimp that increase feed conversion ratios and create better fish health.
>
> Rangen products are sold and used around the world."

Sheriff Scott responded. "Well, that doesn't give us much help, except maybe Casey likes fish!"

They left the city hall parking lot, drove to the stoplight, and turned right on Main Street. It took only a few minutes to drive three blocks, pass several stores, a senior citizens' center, and restaurants, to arrive at the Rangen parking lot. They parked in a visitor parking space and entered what appeared to be the main office. There were several desks scattered around a large room, and they were greeted by an elderly woman sitting at the nearest desk.

She asked, "What can I do for you?"

Sheriff Scott again introduced himself and Harry and requested to see Casey Denney.

The woman glanced around the room as if confirming. "Sheriff, Casey is not here now. He and his wife were on vacation last week, and he was due in this morning. Is there anyone else that can help you?"

Sheriff Scott politely declined the offer and asked, "Could you give us an address where he lives? We need to contact him as soon as possible."

The woman opened a drawer and pulled out what looked like a company directory, scanned the pages, wrote an address on a sticky note, and handed it to Sheriff Scott.

"This is his address. Is there something wrong? It's not like him; he always lets us know if he is not coming in, or if he is going to be late."

"We'll check it out and let you know if we find anything wrong. Thanks for your help."

They headed back to the stoplight, turned right on Broadway, and continued on the road back to Twin Falls. They turned on Fair Street and stopped in front of an attractive, small single-family home with a garage and a carport at the address furnished by the woman at Rangen. A white Jeep was parked in the carport. They approached the front door and rang the doorbell. They could hear the bell ringing, but nobody responded. They rang it again, still no response. They tried the door. It was unlocked, so Sheriff Scott knocked again, only louder, and announced their presence.

"Hello, anyone home? Twin Falls County Sheriff's Department."

No response. Harry announced again, "Twin Falls County Sheriff's Department! Anybody home?"

Still no response.

Suspecting a problem, they decided that they might need a search warrant to proceed. So, just to be on solid legal grounds, they called Sam and instructed her to get a judge to issue a search warrant for the Denney residence. They would be back in the office in twenty or thirty minutes to pick it up.

When they got back at the office, the search warrant was waiting, so they retraced their route back to Buhl and parked in front of the Denney home. Nothing had changed. The Jeep was still in the carport, and the front door was unlocked.

They moved into the house and searched each room. It appeared that no one had been there for some time, and in checking the refrigerator, they found that it was empty and off. The cupboards were also stripped. In checking the garage, they found a Toyota sedan, probably driven by Casey's wife, although they had not bothered to confirm that he was married. Under the circumstances, they had assumed so based on what the lady at Rangen had said. Exiting the house, Sheriff Scott suggested, "Harry, check with the neighbors, and see if they can provide any information. I'll check the mailbox."

The mailbox was stuffed with a few bills and the usual advertising fliers, leading the sheriff to assume that if they had gone out of town for any time, they had not bothered to put a hold on the mail and weren't concerned about paying any bills.

After a few minutes, Harry returned.

"I talked to two neighbors. They said that the couple had been gone for at least a week, and they had not seen the Denneys return. There had not been any activity at the house either, and they said it wasn't like the Denneys to just disappear without letting the neighbors know and asking them to keep an eye on the place."

With a feeling that the mystery was deepening, Sheriff Scott and Harry got back in the cruiser and headed back to Twin Falls, each pondering what was happening. On the ride back, Sheriff Scott used his cell phone to inform Sergeant Hamilton of what they had found and suggested that the Buhl police department keep a close watch on the Denney home and let them know if the Denneys reappeared.

Chapter 7
The Surprise

Casey Denney was the last of five generations with roots in Buhl, Idaho. His great-great-grandfather, Eddie O. Denney, had been one of the original homesteaders that had settled Twin Falls County when, in 1906, the Twin Falls Southside Project introduced irrigation water to the fertile semi-arid land. He farmed a 320-acre tract of land five miles south of Buhl.

Casey's great-grandfather, Glenn T. Denney, grew up on the family farm, graduated from Buhl High School, continued to farm with his father. During World War II, he and his family left the farm, and he worked for Morrison and Knutson as a carpenter in heavy industrial construction. Returning after the war, he used his carpenter skills to open a cabinet shop and build several houses in the Buhl/Castleford area. In fact, Casey and his wife, upon settling in Buhl, lived in one of the houses built in 1983 by his great-grandfather.

Casey's grandfather, Richard G. Denney, was also born in Buhl, graduated from Buhl High School and the University of Idaho, and married his high school sweetheart, Doris Bishop. They lived in many states where Richard worked as a chemical engineer for energy and chemical companies. They spent their last years retired in eastern Tennessee.

Casey's father, Stephen M. Denney, was born in California, where he met his wife, Marie. He completed dental school and two years in the U.S.

Navy before returning to Twin Falls to establish a dental practice. They, however, chose to live in Buhl because of the small-town atmosphere. Upon retiring, they relocated to Park City, Utah, in their ski-in ski-out cabin that the family had enjoyed for many years.

All were good, hard-working, patriotic citizens who prided themselves in following God's laws to the best of their ability and proudly obeying the laws of the land. What education they had received was in schools with teachers that were not afraid to mention God in the classroom and taught and practiced the Judeo-Christian principles that formed the basis for the Constitution and laws of the United States. They appreciated the opportunities that the United States offered to those that were willing to work hard, love and support their families, and defend the nation when called to do so. These principles were handed down to each succeeding generation and formed the basis for Casey Denney's character.

Casey was born in Twin Falls and graduated from Buhl High School, where he was a star football quarterback, basketball point guard, and baseball shortstop. He graduated from the University of Idaho with a degree in agricultural systems management and returned to Buhl to work for Rangen and marry his high school sweetheart, Taylor Hudson. Casey's older brother, Brady, was a PE professor at Southern Adventist University in Collegedale, Tennessee, and his younger sister, Kayla, a music professor at Walla Walla University in Walla Walla, Washington. Both shared Casey's trust in Christ and a commitment to obeying God's commands.

Both Casey and Taylor loved the outdoors and took advantage of the mountain hiking, hunting, and fishing that southern Idaho offered. Casey and Taylor had hoped to have children to add another generation to the family tree. They applied for a maternity permit but had not heard that it had been approved. Casey and Taylor were good Christians, active members of the Twin Falls Seventh-day Adventist Church, and law-abiding citizens that were very diligent about honoring the laws of God and the country—a principle ingrained in them from birth.

Two weeks prior to the day Sheriff Cark and Harry expanded their investigation to Buhl, Casey came home from work at Rangen to find Taylor sitting on their bed, sobbing.

Casey moved into the room, approached the bed, took a seat next to Taylor, and lovingly placed his arm around her shoulder.

"Honey, what's the matter? Is there something you want to tell me?"

Taylor did not respond, but instead dug her head deeper into Casey's chest and sobbed even harder. Casey responded by taking her fully into his embrace and holding her tight against him.

"Now, now, that's all right. You just have a good cry, and we'll get to the bottom of whatever is bothering you when you're ready."

He held her for several minutes, and the sobbing began to subside. Taylor pulled away from Casey, and using the handkerchief she had been holding in her hand, wiped her tear-stained face, gave a big sigh, looked into Casey's eyes, and asked, "Do you love me? Do you really, really love me?"

Not expecting such a request, all he could say was, "Of course I do, I've always loved you and will always love you! Why are you asking?"

"Do you really mean it? Do you really mean that you will always love me?"

Now, feeling the emotion between them, and the deep need that Taylor obviously this moment was dealing with, Casey very softly but convincingly responded.

"Yes, Taylor, I really mean it; I really will always love you!"

"Good. I needed to hear it because I think we have a problem that might strain that love. I'm pregnant. Oh, Casey, I'm so sorry."

Casey was speechless.

Chapter 8
The Plan

Casey rose from the bed, took Taylor by both hands, lifted her to him, and enfolded her in a warm embrace as her sobbing subsided. After several minutes, he led her into the kitchen and took a seat at the kitchen table. Taylor paced the floor and began to cry. Casey rose and took Taylor's trembling hands and gently asked, "Are you sure?"

Taylor shook her head positively. "Oh, Casey, what are we going to do. We will lose our home. We will go to jail. They will kill our baby. Our life is ruined. I'm so sorry. It's my fault. I should have been more careful. Can we still get a permit?"

Casey shook his head." Not likely. From what I hear, permits are not being issued in Twin Falls County and take years to get approved. We probably don't have the time. How long have you known?"

Taylor squeezed his hands tightly. "I had suspicions last month, but this month it became obvious. I think that I am probably at least three months along. Casey, I understand how serious this is and what the consequences are, but I don't believe in abortion. I would never consent to that! And besides, this is our baby, and I want more than anything for us to have this baby, no matter what it takes!"

Casey gathered his thoughts, looked into Taylor's pretty brown eyes that he so loved and appreciated, and responded." Okay, but it is not going to be easy. We will probably lose our home, but they are not taking us to jail, and they are not going to kill our baby. We have to go someplace where no one can find us and leave no trace of how we got there. We can't tell anyone, not even our parents or any of the rest of our family."

"But that's not fair to our parents. They need to know," she sobbed.

No, Taylor! We can't get them involved. Our friends at church can't know either. We have to go away somewhere that no one will think to look. We will have to survive on our own without any outside help for who knows how long."

"But first, we have to figure out how we are going to hide and what we will need. We are tough. We both are experienced campers and hikers. We both are strong and in good health. But the most important thing that we have going for us is our faith in God and our willingness to put our trust in Him. Taylor, with God's help, we are going to make this happen. We are going to get through this together, and we are going to have and keep our child!"

Taylor felt the energy coursing through their hands. "Casey, I also believe that with God's help, we can survive and have our baby, but I am still scared. Let's pray!"

They dropped to their knees, grasped hands, and bowed their heads, and Casey led in prayer.

"Father in heaven, we need You so much. We have always tried to be law-abiding citizens, but this time we put our trust in You and must rebel against a law that goes against Your will. We want to have our baby, and we want to do Your will. Please give us the strength to get through this. Send Your angels to protect and guide us. Give us wisdom to make the right choices. Thank You for loving us and thank You for the blessing that Taylor is carrying. Amen!"

As they rose to their feet, Taylor grasped Casey's hand and declared, "Casey, I love you so much, and I trust you to take care of us, but where can we possibly go so no one will find us and still survive?

Casey had to think for a moment, and then his face lit up, and his smile broadened. "Do you remember that time a couple years ago when we spent a week camping along the South Boise River in the Sawtooth Mountains? Remember, we hiked to Heart Lake."

Taylor nodded in agreement.

"My grandfather Denney told me about it. At Boy Scout camp, he and two friends hiked up to Heart Lake when the Buhl Boy Scout troop was at a camp-o-ree. The next year, he guided two fishermen from Buhl to Heart Lake looking for rainbow trout. Heart Lake is not well known, and besides, it isn't easy making that climb. However, it should be a good place to start, even if we have to search for a more secure hiding place. It has fresh water, lots of berries in season, wild greens, and, of course, fish in the lake. The problem is getting there without anyone knowing about it. Let me think about that for a moment. "

Casey hesitated for a moment and then announced. "I am going into the office and make a list of all the things I think we need and then let you look it over for what other things you think we might need, especially for the birth and care of our baby."

Casey retreated to the office, leaving Taylor alone to digest what had been said and begin formulating a list of her own. He soon emerged with a list of things they would need to survive at Heart Lake, handed it to Taylor, and suggested. "Taylor, have a look, and see if you can think of anything else we might need?"

Casey began to pace the floor as he rapidly expressed his thoughts, talking to no one in particular. "We can take all week to buy what we need, just getting a few things here and there to reduce the chance of anyone getting suspicious of our plans. We can leave next Sunday. I have the next week scheduled for vacation, so that will give time to go away before anyone gets suspicious."

"We won't be able to take one of our vehicles since it will be dead giveaway of where we are, so we will have to get someone to drive us there, someone who can be trusted, and the last person anyone would think to ask."

"I know just the right person. Billy Henry"

Taylor nodded in agreement and turned her attention to the list of supplies. She added baby stuff, reusable diapers, powdered formula, bottles, and nipples, along with a baby birthing kit. "It looks complete to me, but I suggest we either get a book or go online to give us a guide about midwifery. I think you will need it when it comes time for the baby to be delivered."

Casey agreed. "I'll stop at the book store in Twin Falls and see if I can find a midwifery book and also see if they have one on wilderness living."

Chapter 9
A Sabbath Rest

After a busy week of accumulating the supplies necessary for their planned escape, and as their custom was, they rose bright and early Saturday morning, looking forward to a restful and spiritual uplifting Sabbath with their friends at the Twin Falls Seventh-day Adventist (SDA) Church. The Sabbath services began with Sabbath School at 9:30 a.m., followed by worship services at 10:45. Taylor and Casey attended both, and it was ironic that the sermon that particular Sabbath was on the last days before Christ's triumphant return to earth with an emphasis of the hard times Christians will experience during those last days, particularly as related to the conflict between what God commanded and the laws of the land.

It started out as a beautiful late spring day with clear skies and a pleasant temperature, so Taylor and Casey joined a group of friends from the church for a picnic lunch at the park at Shoshone Falls. Shoshone Falls was one of the two natural waterfalls on the Snake River north of Twin Falls. At times of abundant water flow on the river, Shoshone Falls was a spectacular site that attracted young and old. Idaho Power, however, had been permitted to divert the water for power generation, and at times, only a small part of the river flow went over the falls. But on this particular day, the river flow was heavy, and the falls were spectacular. Taylor and Casey and their friends loved to spend Sabbath afternoons there, enjoying the natural beauty and fellowship with fellow church members.

After lunch, Taylor and Casey joined their friends in a circle of camp chairs. The circle included Alisha, Ashley, Kevin, Blair, Megan, Jake, Christie, Sara, and Joe. All with the exception of Christie had been raised in the SDA Church, had attended SDA schools and colleges, but for various reasons had drifted away from their roots. However, upon moving to Twin Falls, they returned to their roots and became active members of the Twin Falls SDA church.

Alisha was in charge of the radiology department at the Twin Falls County Hospital; Ashley owned a restaurant in Twin Falls; Kevin owned one of the drug stores in Twin Falls; Blair was president of the largest bank in Twin Falls, and Megan worked from home as part-owner of a medical billing service. All five had relocated from Chicago because of the chaos and rising increase in crime there.

Jake and Christie came to Twin Falls from Austin, Texas. Jake was a CRNA at the Twin Falls Clinic, where Ray King also worked. Christie was also part-owner of the same medical billing service as Megan. They had two daughters, Sloane and Savanah, who, along with Sara and Joe's two daughters, Ashlynn and Brinlee, were busy trying to catch one of the butterflies that were flitting around the park.

Sara and Joe came from Charlotte, North Carolina, to Twin Falls for Joe to be the manager of a new research & development facility. Sara was the third owner of the medical billing service company. Sara and Joe, as well as Jake and Christie, had their children before the worldwide birth restrictions became law. The others claimed that they wished they would have had children before the ban, but had all expressed their willingness to refrain from attempting to have children and were resigned to a childless existence.

After several minutes of small talk, there was a pause in the conversation, and Joe spoke up. "What do you think about the pastor's sermon today; how close are we to Jesus' return?"

Kevin immediately answered him. "I don't see how much longer this earth can stand the turmoil around us. Just look at what is happening right now in Chicago. It's a mess with all the killings and other crimes. How long will it be before that cancer spreads to the rest of the country? Twin Falls may seem like a safe haven now, but how long before we start experiencing that here?"

Ashley agreed. "Also, look what is happening in the rest of the world. Countries are developing their own nuclear weapons and building great armies. For what? Certainly not their own defense? The world may destroy itself before He can return."

Jake chimed in. "We left Austin for two reasons. One, the city just got too big, traffic was terrible, and even there the crime rate was increasing, and two, it seemed to be getting hotter and hotter in the summertime. Maybe there is something to this global warming scare."

Ever the skeptic, Blair offered his opinion. "I don't believe all this hype that claims that unless we change our ways, global warming will destroy the planet. I believe that God is powerful enough to create the universe and this earth and is powerful enough and smart enough to have also created earth's atmosphere to be self-correcting, knowing that we would need all this carbon dioxide-producing energy in the last days to spread the gospel to the world."

Pausing to make sure the others were listening, Blair continued. "The world, as we know it, may be destroyed in our lifetime, but it will not be because of global warming. It will be because Jesus returns. And another thing, I think this population control movement that bans having children unless you have the proper permit is wrong, and I wish there were something we could do about it. Why is it that more and more, we are asked to pick and choose between God's laws and man's laws?"

Megan, Blair's wife, who seldom offered a controversial opinion, joined the discussion." I agree with Blair that the ban is unfair. Blair and I had purposely waited to have a child until we were more secure in our relationship, and now that it's the right time, we can't. It's just not fair!"

Ashley looked at Megan and kindly offered," Megan, I feel for you and agree that it's not fair, but it doesn't impact Kevin and me as much as you since we had decided to not have a family because of our concern that Jesus is coming soon, and we would not want our child to go through the time of trouble just before He returns. There may be times of persecution and hardship because of our faith, and it will be tough enough for Kevin and me to endure. We would hate to see a child have to suffer the same. But that is our choice, and I respect your point of view as well."

Alisha made an attempt to lighten the conversation. "I don't have to worry because I'll probably always be the just the loveable "aunt" to all of your kids. One day at a time is my philosophy, you know, que sera, sera."

Sara, Joe's wife, expressed her relief. "I'm just glad we had our girls when we did, but I hate to think what may be in store for them. It was bad enough when I grew up, but what will it be like for them?"

Christie, Jake's wife, offered the same sentiments." I agree with Sara. I would be afraid to have any more children even if we could get a permit. I also agree with Blair. It seems like there is more and more pressure to abandon God's laws in favor of man's laws. Didn't God command us to be fruitful and populate the earth?"

> *It seems like there is more and more pressure to abandon God's laws in favor of man's laws.*

Joe returned to the conversation. "Think about this! We keep hearing reports and rumors that the mainstream churches in the US are banding together to try to get a national "Sunday Law" passed in Congress. We know that such a law would require worshiping on Sunday by all and greatly penalize people like us who honor God's law by remembering the Sabbath, Saturday. Are we going to be strong enough to buck the system and remain faithful to God's law?"

The rest were unanimous in agreeing that with God's help, they could. But Blair further cautioned the group. "The Sabbath and Sunday laws are big issues, but remember that Jesus told us in Matthew 24 that there would be other problems before He returned: deception, wars and rumors of wars, nation against nation, famines, pestilences, earthquakes, sorrows, affliction, and killing of those who obey God's laws, betrayal, hatred of others, iniquity everywhere, and a void of love one to another. But we have hope that if we do endure with God's help, He will save us."

Taylor and Casey listened quietly to the conversation going on around them, and both later confided that they felt both sadness and dread. They so wanted to let their friends know that Taylor was pregnant, but reluctantly held it all inside, knowing that this group would probably be some of the first asked about where to find them. It would be best if their friends knew as little as possible about their plans or concerns. They were also concerned about how long they could survive in the wilderness with the turmoil in the world, but they still had a full measure of faith in their God, that He would see them through this.

The afternoon flew by, and the group moved on to other topics of conversation. Although they tried diligently, the four girls did not catch a butterfly. Soon, it became obvious that it was time to go. The group parted with a round of hugs and promises to see each other next Sabbath. The sky that had been clear that morning had turned cloudy and dark in the west as if to mirror some of their thoughts of impending trouble

Taylor and Casey drove silently back to Buhl, each lost in their own thoughts of what tomorrow had in store and sadness that they may never see their dear friends again.

Chapter 10
Escape

Casey and Taylor awoke at 4:30 Sunday morning from a restless and troubled sleep at the shrill, unwelcome sound of the alarm on their nightstand. They quickly showered, dressed, and ate a breakfast from what little food they had left in the house. They had just finished the little bit of packing they had left when the doorbell rang. Casey answered the door. It was Billy Henry, right on time, and ready to drive them to their destination.

Billy Henry was the most trusted man in town. He ran a successful dry-cleaning business but, on the side, cleaned most of the major businesses in town. He had a key to all of their doors, and the business owners had full trust in his honesty. Billy was a quiet person that went about his business in an efficient and professional manner. No one really knew much about where he came from or if he even had a family. One day, he just appeared alongside his great-uncle, known, by the people of Buhl, as simply Henry. Henry took Billy under his wing, and the two of them maintained the business that Henry had built. When Henry died, Billy stepped in and continued to clean all the businesses in Buhl, saved his money, and opened the dry-cleaning business.

No one in Buhl knew where Henry came from either. One day, he just showed up, and the legend was that he got tired of working for the Union

Pacific Railroad and rode a train to the end of the line. Buhl was the end of the line for the Idaho Short Line, a branch of the Union Pacific.

Henry opened a shoe-shine parlor in a small storefront on Broadway next to the Idaho First National Bank. He approached the manager of the bank one day and asked if he could have the job of cleaning the bank. From that humble beginning, Henry expanded his cleaning business to include most of the stores, banks, and office buildings and became a very rich and most trusted man in Buhl. He continued to shine shoes during the day and clean businesses at night. Although no one knew for sure, it was rumored that Henry helped many of the poorer kids in Buhl get a college education. Those who received his help were sworn to secrecy. Billy was one of those that received Henry's help not only educationally but having his character, work ethic, and unquestionable loyalty shaped by the elder Henry.

Casey was sure that, if anyone could keep their secret, Billy Henry could and was the one he now trusted to help them disappear. He greeted Billy with a hug.

Billy gave Casey a return hug and greeted Taylor, who had been standing behind Casey.

Casey declared. "Good morning, Billy, we are all packed and ready to go. Are you sure you are okay with this? I know we didn't give you much information about where we are going or why. You will just have to trust us. We appreciate your willingness to help us. All you need to do is go with us, help unload the Jeep, bring it back to Buhl, and park it in the carport. Are you still okay with that?"

Billy replied, "Of course, I'm okay with that, and I don't have to know anything else. I'm just here to help a friend as God would want me to do, plain and simple. Now, let's get on the road. I don't know where we are going, but I suspect it is not just around the corner."

Without any more delay, they got in the Jeep. Casey drove with Billy in the front passenger seat, and Taylor curled up with a blanket and a pillow to catch some more sleep.

Buhl was dark. There was a dog barking in the distance, but all else was quiet. Casey had a small knot in his stomach and some regret as they left their home. He knew they were doing the only thing they could do, and it seemed right. As they turned right on Main Street and headed for Clear Lakes Road, he remembered that he had neglected to lock the front door. Too late now, but it didn't really matter anyway.

They continued on Clear Lake Road and crossed the Snake River. They passed through the small towns of Wendell and Gooding and headed for the small town of Fairfield, where they stopped at a convenience store/service station to stretch their legs, get gas, and purchase a small snack. Fairfield is the county seat of Camas County.

Leaving Fairfield, they turned right on to North Soldier Road toward the Sawtooth Mountain Wilderness. They continued north, intersecting with Fleck Summit Road, and after traveling for miles and two and a half hours, they passed the Methodist Youth Camp. They continued on Fleck Summit Road and South Boise Road for another ten miles where it dead-ended on the bank of the South Boise River.

It was a beautiful setting with the clear waters of the South Boise River flowing swiftly across smooth boulders. Wildflowers were blooming up the slopes bordering the river, and there was a gentle breeze rustling through the many aspen and evergreen trees along the banks.

Casey, Taylor, and Billy got out of Jeep, stretched their legs, and for a few moments, just stood there in silence, taking in the beautiful example of God's creation. Casey suggested that they thank God for a safe journey, so they all knelt on the carpet of green beside the river, and Casey offered a prayer.

"Thank You, God, for giving us a safe journey. Thank You for creating such beauty for us to enjoy. Give us strength to face the days ahead. Protect us from danger and deliver us to Your kingdom when You return. Give Billy a safe trip back to Buhl. Also, give comfort to our family and friends as they realize that we have disappeared. Thank You for being our friend, Savior, and God. We pray these things in Jesus' name. Amen."

They unloaded the Jeep. It took the three of them several trips to get all the supplies and gear up the two-and-a-third miles to the proposed campsite, which was about a half-mile below Heart Lake. By four in the afternoon, they had moved all of the gear and supplies to a level, grassy spot along the small stream that tumbled down the rocky slope from the lake. The site was sheltered by several evergreen trees and seemed to have an abundance of dead wood scattered around the area, ideal for burning in a campfire.

After the last trip, they gave Billy a big hug, thanked him for all his help, and repeated instruction as to what to do with the Jeep upon his return to Buhl. Casey offered Billy some money for his help, but as he expected, Billy refused.

They were saddened as they watched him disappear down the trail, realizing that they might never see him again or anyone else for that matter. It was a lonely feeling, but they soon busied themselves getting the camp set up and securing the supplies. By sundown, they had pitched a small two-person mountain tent and secured the rest of the supplies. As they lay beside each other, listening to the night sounds and the gentle melody of the stream passing, the tension of the day and the concerns for the future seemed to drift away with the gathering of a restful sleep.

Chapter 11

A New Day

They awoke the next morning with the first glow of light in the east. As they stretched out the stiff muscles that had been taxed to their limit the day before, they again marveled at the beauty around them. It promised to be a beautiful, cloudless day, with pleasant temperatures. They still had work to do to expand the camp into a more livable site, but first things first. They held each other and prayed.

"God, again, we love You and appreciate You for bringing us to this safe and serene spot. Please bless the new life that is growing in Taylor, and give us the courage, wisdom, and strength to properly and safely deliver, protect, and nourish it to one day follow and serve You. Amen"

After a light breakfast, they changed into their hiking clothes and headed up the stream to explore the lake. The trail was a lot steeper than they had experienced the day before, and at times, hardly discernible from the surrounding terrain, but they were able to finally crest the last few feet and gaze in wonder at the clear, blue lake stretching before them. It was shaped like a heart. The banks were barren of any trees, shrubs, or flowers.

They walked around the right side of the lake to a small peninsula that jutted into the lake, giving it the shape of a heart. They ventured out on the peninsula that appeared to have been formed by a rock slide from the shear slope up to the top of the basin. At the end of the peninsula, they peered into the deep blue water, and to their wonder, could clearly see the bottom and small fish swimming lazily below them. There was still a bank of snow above the lake, even though it was late spring, and several small trickles of water from the melting snow cascaded down into the lake, replenishing the lake water and allowing the overflow to enter the stream by their campsite. Again, they marveled at the way God had created a constant and sustainable supply of water for their daily needs.

They explored the left side of the lake, finding it to be much like the right side, and then stopped and sat down on a big boulder near the start of the stream. After a few minutes, Casey broke the silence. "Well, sweetheart, what do you think—can we survive here? We may be here for a very long time. Do you think we made a mistake?"

Taylor knew her husband well, and by his tone of voice and the concern in his eyes that what he was really asking was, could she really survive in this isolated, potentially harsh wilderness for an indefinite time? He knew he could, but he wasn't sure about her.

> *They marveled at the way God had created a constant and sustainable supply of water for their daily needs.*

Taylor gently squeezed his hand, looked into his eyes, and replied, "I think I am up to the challenge. After all, women were created to survive and bear children, so don't you worry about me. Besides, I plan to rely on strength and perseverance from God, and I know He will provide my every need!"

She poked him in the ribs and kissed his cheek. "So you, big boy, worry about yourself, and don't worry about me! I'll be fine."

Reassured, he playfully tousled her hair and grabbed her hand. "Okay, then, let's get back to camp and get to work making our new home."

The weather cooperated. Each morning, they arose to find the temperature ideal for the hard work they faced. The sky was clear and cloudless, and the sun shone brightly. They discovered an abundance of downed lodgepole pine trees lying about that were just the right size to use as building lumber. They constructed a twenty-foot by twenty-foot log cabin complete with a thatched roof of layered pine boughs over a forest-green tarp that they had carried up the trail.

Hopefully, the pine boughs and green tarp would blend in with the surrounding pine trees and be relatively invisible from the air. At some time, they fully expected that someone would be searching for them, most likely, initially from the air.

They placed their air mattress and sleeping bags on a raised platform on one end of the room. On the other end, they built another raised platform (shelf) to hold all their other supplies. The cracks between the logs were sealed by mud from the stream banks, and the rustic cabin even had an opening, facing the stream, for a makeshift door hung by three leather-strap hinges.

They fashioned a table from the lodgepole pine in the grove of trees that also had side benches for sitting for a meal and an enclosed water tower rigged to hold a bucket and hose above their heads for showering. If they left the cold water from the stream in the bucket long enough, the sun and heat of the day warmed the water enough, so it was not a terrible shock to take a shower before going to bed. This would work fine in the summer heat, but they would have to go to plan B when winter came—spit baths from water heated over an open fire.

By Friday afternoon, they had completed most of the structures from the lodgepole pine that would serve as their home. Late in the afternoon, they searched the area for edible plants and berries and gathered enough to last for the weekend. Included were several sego lily bulbs and flowers that were in full bloom along with wild gooseberries and huckleberries. At sundown, they welcomed the Sabbath as a break in the week's hectic activity.

All had gone according to plan so far. They were secure and safe with shelter and enough supplies to make it through the winter. Except for Billy, no one knew where they were. Even though they had each other, they shared a feeling of loneliness. They, however, both had their steadfast faith in God, and for the moment, that was sufficient.

After a restful night's sleep, they awoke to a new day of the wonder of God's creation surrounding them. The sun rising in the east cast a bright golden hue to the bare limestone peak above them. Birds sang in the tall pines, and chipmunks scurried here and there, searching for fresh seeds or pine nuts. They studied their Bibles for a while as the sound of the rushing stream created a melodious background to the ever-changing sounds of the forest. The sounds from the forest, the gentle breeze, the babbling stream, and the birds in the air seemed to be saying in harmony, "God is good all the time! All the time, God is good!"

Chapter 12
The Investigation

Officer Hamilton replaced the phone on his desk after assuring Sheriff Scott that he would check on the Denneys' home and at Rangen during the week and keep him informed of any new developments. He made a mental note to stop by the Denney home tomorrow and made a notation in his day planner to do so at least once or twice a day for the rest of the week. He did not have a clue as to what was going on but considered it professional courtesy to cooperate with the sheriff.

On Tuesday morning, he found the Jeep still in the driveway, and the house still unlocked as reported by Sheriff Scott on Monday. He checked with Rangen, and Casey still had not shown up for work.

He found the same thing on Wednesday, Thursday, and Friday. On Friday afternoon, he called the sheriff's office.

"Sheriff Scott, this is Officer Hamilton of the Buhl Police Department. I checked on the Denney home each day this week and found no one home, no evidence that anyone had been there, and the Jeep was still in the carport. I also checked with Rangen, and Casey Denney has not returned to work. Is there anything else you want me to do? Should I keep checking?"

Sheriff Scott showed no surprise. "Officer Hamilton, thanks for the report. Yes, keep checking and report any change. We will be in touch if we need any further assistance, but in the meantime, you might check with some of the people in Buhl who may know them and see if they can shed some light on where they might be.

Officer Hamilton replied, "I have already made a few contacts in Buhl, including some of the Rangen employees, and one of them told me that Casey and Taylor were members of the Twin Falls Seventh-day Adventist Church. Maybe the pastor or some of their close friends from the church can provide some information. I think it would be worth checking."

"I agree. Thanks for the lead. We appreciate your help. Have a great day."

After hanging up the phone, Sheriff Scott summoned his three deputies into his office and relayed the report from the Buhl Police.

"I think we should treat this as a missing person case with the possibility of foul play. Tom, I want you to file a missing person report and put out an APB to all the law enforcement agencies in Southern Idaho, including the state police. Include the license number of their Jeep, and see if Officer Hamilton in Buhl can get a good picture of the two of them to include in the APB."

He then turned to Harry Mason. "Harry, I want you to visit the pastor of the Twin Falls Seventh Day Church and see if he has any information about where they might be. Also, ask him for some names of their friends so that we can contact them too. Harry, do you know anything about their parents? We should also contact them."

Harry replied, "I don't know anything about their parents, but I'll make some calls and see if I can find out anything."

Harry and Tom retreated to their offices. Phil remained in Scott's office. "Is there anything you want me to do?"

Sheriff Scott thought for a moment. "Not now, Phil. We need to be free to respond to other needs. I'm concerned that we are spending too much time on the Denney case anyway. If we don't get some answers soon, we may need to bring in some outside help, like the FBI. After all, the only evidence we have, slim though it is, points to a possible federal case."

Sheriff Scott hated the thought that he might need to involve the FBI. If this investigation did involve an unpermitted pregnancy, he was in conflict between his duties as a law officer, a parent, and a human being. He always tried to uphold the law, but he also had sympathy for any young couple who wanted to have a family.

His conflicting thoughts were interrupted by Harry returning to his office and declaring, "Sheriff, I located Casey Denney's parents. They live in Park City, Utah. Here is their address."

Sheriff Scott accepted the piece of paper offered by Harry and examined it.

"Good job, I'll have my daughter in Salt Lake make a visit to them and see if she can get a statement. You go visit the Seventh-day Adventist pastor."

Harry left the office and headed for his car.

Sheriff Scott picked up the phone and soon had his step-daughter on the line. "Chelsea, this is your dad. I need a favor. I'll text you an address. I need you to visit a couple in Park City. I need to reach their son and daughter-in-law to ask them some questions. Ask them if they know where they are. Try not to alarm them, just say a friend of yours in Twin Falls would like to get in touch with them."

"Okay, Dad, how soon do you need the information?"

"As soon as you can make the visit. I know you are busy, but I would appreciate you contacting them. I don't want to needlessly alarm them. I think they would be more concerned if I contacted them. I know you will keep it low-key. How are things going?"

Chelsea and her dad chatted a few more minutes about the weather in Salt Lake and her recent experiences at the newspaper and then agreed to get together real soon. Both hung up, knowing it would be a while before that happened.

Later in the afternoon, Tom came into Sheriff Scott's office with a draft of the APB.

"Sheriff, here is a draft of the APB for your approval. I contacted Officer Hamilton in Buhl, and he went to the Denneys' home and found recent photos. He scanned and sent them to me, and they are included."

Sheriff Scott read the APB draft and returned it to Tom. "Looks good, Tom; send it out!"

They hadn't heard from Harry by quitting time, so they all left, hoping to get a report from him tomorrow.

The next morning at staff meeting, Harry reported: "I visited with the Seventh-day Adventist Church pastor, and he said he had no idea why the Denneys were not in Buhl. He had seen them a couple weeks ago at the Saturday church services, and they seemed normal and fine. He gave me the names of two of their close friends. I managed to see them last evening, and they did not have any useful information either. I guess I drew a blank. They all agreed, though, that Casey and Taylor were devout Christians as well as good, law-abiding citizens."

> *They all agreed, though, that Casey and Taylor were devout Christians as well as good, law-abiding citizens.*

"Good work, Harry! I guess we are at a dead end. Let's wait a few more days to see if Chelsea has a chance to contact the parents."

With that, they left the staff meeting and returned to their offices to concentrate on other duties.

Chapter 13
The Parents

The next week a well-dressed, middle-aged couple stormed into the sheriff's office and demanded to see Sheriff Scott. Sam politely asked, "Who shall I say wishes to speak to him?"

The man quickly and rather gruffly replied, "I am Steven Denney, and this is my wife, Marie. We are Casey Denney's parents, and we are here to get some answers."

Sam politely suggested they take a seat and offered them something to drink. They declined a drink and moved to the offered chairs.

"I'll tell Sheriff Scott you are here to see him."

She retreated to Sheriff Scott's office, closed the door, and reported. "Sheriff, Casey Denney's parents are here to see you, and I don't think they are too happy about something. Shall I show them in?"

"By all means, send them in!"

Sam returned to the reception area and approached Mr. and Mrs. Denney. "Follow me. Sheriff Scott will see you now."

Sheriff Scott shook their hands and started the conversation. "I am Sheriff Scott, what can I do for you?"

It didn't take long for the man to respond.

"I am Steven Denney, and this is my wife, Marie. We are Casey Denney's parents, and we just want to know what is going on. A few days ago, a young lady from the Salt Lake Tribune came by our house in Park City, asking about how to get in touch with our son and his wife. She said some friends wanted to get in touch with them. We gave her their address and telephone number. She also asked if we had recently heard from them? We had not. What is—"

Sheriff Scott interrupted. "That was my daughter. I asked her to make the contact."

Steven Denney continued. "That makes it more of a puzzle. Well, anyway, we tried calling Casey and got no answer. We then called the pastor of the church here in Twin Falls that Casey and Taylor attend and asked him what was going on. He told us that one of your deputies had been by asking some questions about Casey and Taylor. What is going on, Sheriff? Are Casey and Taylor in some kind of trouble?"

"Have you been by your son's house in Buhl?"

"No, we were on our way there but decided to stop by here to see what you had to say."

Sheriff Scott continued. "Well, a few days ago, we checked with the Buhl police department, visited with the people at Rangen's, and went by your son's house. Your son had not returned to work after his week's vacation, and the house was wide open with the Jeep in the carport and the Honda in the garage. There was no evidence of foul play. The front door was unlocked, and as far as we could determine, nothing had been stolen or vandalized. The Buhl police department went by the house and checked with Rangen's all that next week, but your son never returned to work, nor did anyone come back to the house. The neighbors were no help either. That's when we decided to make contact with you and the church pastor."

Mrs. Denney spoke up. "Sheriff, what do you think this all means?"

"We don't have any real proof, but we suspect that your daughter-in-law may be pregnant without the required permit, and they may have fled to hide from the authorities to escape the consequences. Keep in mind this is only what we suspect, and we have no real proof. They are probably just two scared kids wanting to be out of sight and out of mind for a while."

Mrs. Denney thought for a minute and then offered, "That is not like them. They would never knowingly break the law, and besides, we are a close and supportive family. Why would they purposely not let us know so we could work it out together? What do you think we should do?"

Sheriff Scott paused and then suggested, "Secure your son's house and take care of everything to preserve their possessions. Then go back to Park City and wait for them to contact you. If you do hear from them, please let us know. "

The Denneys agreed and left. Sheriff Scott picked up the phone and called the FBI.

Chapter 14
The Mountain Lions

The days of summer flew by, and Casey and Taylor settled into a daily and weekly routine. They awoke to the sound of birds singing in the trees, and the sun rays creeping down the side of the mountain above them. They freshened themselves with a quick dousing of cold water from the stream to sleepy faces. The pregnancy had progressed without any complications, and by late August, she had passed the six-month mark, and her expanding stomach was proof enough.

Before breakfast, they sat at their makeshift table, had prayer thanking God for keeping them safe one more day, and studied the Bible. The days were still hot. Several times a week, after a breakfast of fresh berries and greens mixed with sego lily bulbs, they liked to hike up to Heart Lake to spend most of the day swimming in the clear, cool water and relaxing along the rocky shore. There were still a few remnants of snowdrifts from the previous winter that were slowly melting into the lake, keeping it and the stream supplied with a continuous source of fresh water.

Casey loved to fish, and the lake was full of pan-size rainbow trout. This particular day, the fish were biting, and as soon as he cast his bait into the water, he had a fish. Maybe it was the bait he was using. On the way up to the lake, they had collected a supply of deer fly larvae from the stream. Deer fly larvae are aquatic and can be found attached to rocks or stream banks just below the surface of the water. Fish love them, so it is no wonder that Casey caught so many fish.

The female Sawtooth Mountains deer fly is a pest to animals and man. They love the blood. A deer fly bite can be very painful. The more Casey fished, the fewer female deer flies there were around to bite. Fortunately, Casey and Taylor had also brought some repellent to keep the pesky deer flies away.

Most of the fish Casey caught were removed from the hook and turned loose back into the lake, particularly the small ones. By mid-afternoon, he had saved three good-sized trout that they would cook over an open fire for their evening meal.

Taylor had been sitting on a big rock near the entrance to the stream. She found enjoyment, comfort, and admiration in her husband's fishing talents and his apparent enjoyment of being here surrounded by the mountains he loved. Periodically, she felt a stirring inside her that reassured her that all was well with their baby.

Her peaceful spell was suddenly broken as she sensed movement to the right and up on the rocky slope above the lake. She slowly turned her head to see what had moved, and she spotted two mountain lions slowly making their way around them to the stream and the trail that led back to their camp.

Taylor turned her head slowly toward Casey and whispered. "Casey, we have visitors."

Casey did not respond. He was in the middle of a cast when Taylor whispered, and the splash of the hook into the lake had muffled Taylor's concerned announcement.

Being as quiet as she could, Taylor slid down from her perch on the big rock and made her way slowly to where Casey stood. She gently touched his shoulder and whispered into his ear, "Casey, there are two mountain lions over to the right heading down the slope toward the stream."

Sensing her alarm, Casey slowly wound his fishing line back to shore and turned to face the trail behind them at the same time gently nudging Taylor behind him. "Taylor, you are right. I see them! They are two adult mountain lions. Be very quiet and don't move."

As they quietly watched, the two big cats approached and crossed the stream about fifty yards from Casey and Taylor. The biggest one slowly turned its head up the stream and appeared to search the trail above. The smaller one took up a position beside the bigger one, and it, too, turned to look up the trail.

Casey and Taylor froze. They had no place to hide and no place to run. They were trapped. They did not have a weapon of any kind to defend themselves, no gun, no club, and the fishing pole Casey clutched in his hand would not be any good against a big mountain lion. Casey recalled the story of Daniel in the lion's den and hoped that God would spare them as he had spared Daniel. Casey clutched Taylor's hand and admonished her again to remain still and quiet.

Time seemed to stand still. Casey and Taylor remained motionless, and so did the big cats. Suddenly the biggest cat raised his head high and let out a blood-curdling roar. The smaller cat shook his head from side to side and joined in with what sounded like a scream. The roar and scream were amplified by the mountain walls as they echoed from one side to the other. Casey squeezed Taylor's hand even harder. He could feel Taylor shudder as she tried to get closer to him.

> *Suddenly the biggest cat raised his head high and let out a blood-curdling roar.*

The two cats hesitated for a moment, turned as if to head down the trail, but then turned suddenly, and with tails held high and louder roars, dashed toward the trembling pair. They menacingly ran to within a few feet of Casey and Taylor and stopped suddenly. Their tails dropped, and they swung their heads from side to side in confusion as their eyes darted from left to right. It was as if Taylor and Casey were no longer there.

Just as suddenly, the two cats turned and headed down the trail. It was if they had seen something or someone more powerful. As they passed the cabin, they hesitated, turned back up the hill, and gave a mighty defiant roar as if to give a stern warning: "This is still our canyon, and don't you forget it."

Casey and Taylor planned to do just that. They would never forget the fright and terror they felt, nor the relief that came knowing that God was still in control and that by His mercy and grace, they were spared for another day.

Still trembling, they embraced to steady their nerves and headed down the trail to the comfort of the cabin. Fishing was over for that day.

That night, in their prayers, they again thanked God for sending His angels to protect them.

Chapter 15
Nature Provides a Way

It was not long after the encounter with the mountain lions that they had another close call.

Again, they were at the lake on another hot fall day, swimming and fishing, and just enjoying being together. The cares of the world seemed so far, far away. Casey had caught a good number of rainbow trout, and Taylor had busied herself with weaving some long leaves of water plants into a mat. She had no use in mind for the mat. She just enjoyed making something out of the plants that had grown at the lake during the warm days of summer. The hollow stems from water plants were of no use in making the mat, so she discarded them beside her on the bank. The weaving occupied her time between an occasional kick from the baby growing inside her, and the humming of a familiar tune seemed to extend the time between kicks.

At first, Taylor thought she heard someone else humming with her, perhaps Casey, as he put more bait on his hook for another cast. No, the sound came from far off, and it was more like a steady hum without a tune. She walked over to where Casey was intent on catching another fish and gently touched his free arm. "Casey, do you hear that hum?"

"What hum?"

"That hum. It seems to be toward the south."

Casey laid his fishing rod on the ground and cupped his hands to his ears. "I think I hear what you mean. You're right—it's definitely a hum."

"What do you think it is? questioned Taylor.

"Beats me! Probably nothing to worry about!"

Casey turned to retrieve his rod and resume fishing, but stopped in his tracks and listened intently. He could distinctly hear the hum, but as he continued to listen, intermixed with the hum was a steady, "whump, whump, whump." As he listened, the sound became louder and louder.

"Taylor, I think that noise is coming from a helicopter, and it is definitely heading in our direction. We need to get back to the cabin."

Then they spotted the helicopter as it turned to come up the canyon.

"No time to get to the cabin. We have to hide."

"But, Casey, there is no place to hide, no trees, no bushes, no rocks big enough to hide behind."

"Right, but we can't just stand here. We'll be spotted for sure. I was afraid this might happen."

"Casey, I have an idea. Take off your clothes."

"What? Take off my clothes?"

"We've no time to argue. Take off your clothes!"

With that, Taylor shed her own clothes and grabbed two of the hollow stems from the water plants she had used to fashion the mat. "Here, take one of these. Get in the water near the water plants and lay under the surface. You can breathe through the hollow stem."

Taylor slid into the water, turned over onto her back, placed the hollow stem into her mouth, and settled to the shallow bottom of the lake. Casey crammed all their clothes in the backpack, hid the backpack behind a big rock out of sight from the lake, and, a bit bewildered, followed her lead. He reached for her hand and squeezed it tightly.

They had barely settled under the water when they looked up and saw the green, gold, and white helicopter of the Idaho Department of Fish and Game appear over the southern rim of the lake. It hovered for a moment and then settled over the center of the lake. As they watched, a large red and black bag descended from the belly of the helicopter. The bag hung just above the surface of the lake for a few moments, and then the bottom of the bag opened, and a cone of water full of fish dropped into the lake.

A few minutes later, the bag was pulled up into the helicopter. With the bag retrieved, the helicopter turned to the right, away from where Casey and Taylor lay and headed back down the canyon. Taylor and Casey stayed under the water quietly for a few more minutes, even though some of the new fish had found their way to them and were nibbling at their exposed bodies. When they were sure the helicopter was gone, they sat up, threw the hollow stems into the water, looked at each other, and started laughing as they playfully splashed each other with water. The nibbling fish retreated.

That night they again thanked God for giving them a way out, using His creation.

Chapter 16
An Unwelcome Visitor

The days grew shorter and shorter. Fall was in the air. The mornings were cooler and crisper, and some mornings the leaves were covered with frost. The aspen trees turned to a bright yellow, and with a gentle wind, the groves were a shimmering blaze of gold.

A morning fire was a pleasant beginning of each new day and soon began to be an absolute necessity. Casey and Taylor constantly scrounged for suitable firewood. Fortunately, they had planned ahead and had an abundant supply of matches and a few butane lighters that made building a fire easy. The challenge was to find and keep a ready supply of seasoned, dry firewood. The occasional rainstorm did not help, and when fall progressed into winter, it would become even harder to find dry wood under the anticipated snow.

One morning, Casey commented, "We need to stockpile some dry wood in the cabin."

Taylor agreed, and soon they were down the trail in search of dry, dead wood. The weather cooperated, and in a few days, they had a huge pile of dry wood stacked along one wall of the cabin. They would use as much other wood as they could find for the morning fires and save the stockpiled wood for starting a fire and absolute emergencies.

Pleased with their work, they thanked God for blessing them with an abundance of dry firewood and asked Him for guidance in managing it efficiently. The next few days were rather uneventful as they followed their established routine. All was peaceful. The mountain lions never returned, and there had not been any sign of any other unwanted visitors that might pose a threat to their existence.

It seemed as if each day, there was something that needed to be modified, rebuilt, or added to their wilderness home. One week, they fashioned a heat reflector on one side of the open firepit. Another day, they were occupied with improving the muddy seal between the logs of the cabin. At least once a week, they replaced the pine boughs on the roof to keep them fresh. Between tasks they explored the canyon and then ventured to the adjoining canyons. A day did not go by that did not include studying the Bible and reflecting on how good God was.

They went to bed that night and tightly held each other, secure in their love for each other and the strength that each had developed so far in their wilderness experience. With a "Good night" and mutual "I love you," they drifted off to sleep.

In the early morning hours, as the sun began to cast its light into the cabin, Taylor stirred and moved as close to Casey as possible, considering the growing child within her, and whispered, "Casey, are you awake? I'm cold. It must be freezing outside."

Still half asleep, Casey responded by getting up and sitting on the edge of the bed. "I guess it's time to start a fire. You stay in bed until I get it going."

He stretched his long arms over his head, yawned, and put on his clothes that had been hung on the wall. They were warm last night when he hung them up, but now they caused him to shiver as he zipped up his down jacket. He slipped into his insulated boots and moved across the floor to the woodpile. He reached for some of the small dry pieces of wood that he planned to use to start the fire.

Taylor watched him move across the room and moved into the warm spot in the bed that Casey had just vacated when she heard a loud hiss followed by Casey yelling, "Ouch!"

She looked up and saw Casey wildly shaking his right hand, and there, at his feet, was a large, coiled snake. She yelled. "Casey! What happened? Did that snake bite you?"

As Casey moved away from the woodpile, he motioned to Taylor to stay away. "Stay in bed. Yes, a snake bit me when I reached for a piece of wood."

"What kind of snake is it? Is it a rattlesnake?"

She knew that a rattlesnake bite could be fatal, and they had little to counteract the venom, except for the old method of making small slices in the skin and sucking the venom out— a task she was not looking forward to.

Casey didn't answer! He moved to the bed, sat down next to Taylor, and grabbed his hand. "Man, it hurts!"

Blood began to seep out of the two holes in his skin. He let the wound bleed. Bleeding would tend to clean the wound of any toxins. After letting it bleed for a minute or two, Casey applied pressure to the wound to stop the bleeding. The pain had eased, and he turned to Taylor and asked. "What was your question?"

Still very upset, Taylor repeated her question. "Was it a rattlesnake?"

"No, I don't think it is a rattlesnake. It likes to pretend it is with its similar markings, aggressive coiling, and ability to flatten out its head into a triangular shape to mimic the shape of a rattlesnake's head. But it lacks one important feature. It doesn't have a rattle. Have you heard a rattle?"

Taylor had to admit that she had not, but a shiver ran through her body as she remembered how she felt when the snake headed out the door.

Casey continued. "I am reasonably sure that it is a bull snake. They are usually rather tame and docile. I must have startled it. One year at Boy Scout camp, we caught a bull snake about that size, and one guy carried it around his neck all day with the head and tail stuffed inside his shirt. The snake evidently enjoyed it because it didn't bite him."

"We even played a trick on one of the new kids by stuffing the snake inside his camera case. He really freaked out when he opened the case."

"Anyway, I think I will be okay as long as I don't get an infection."

With that, he gathered an armload of wood and left to get a fire going.

Chapter 17
The Move

"When you go through deep waters and great trouble, I will be with you. When you go through rivers of difficulty, you will not drown!" (Isa. 43:2–3, TLB).

The days got shorter, and the nights grew colder. It soon began to snow, and the ground was covered by a shimmering white blanket. It became harder and harder to find enough food, so they began to delve into the supply of dried meals that, until now, had not been touched.

After a particularly cold night, Taylor could not hold back any longer. With a touch of fear and a lot of concern in her voice, she confronted Casey.

"Casey, we need to talk. I am worried that we will not be able to survive the winter here in the cabin as we planned. I am also concerned about having our child in this environment and weather. I know it will be due soon, and frankly, I'm scared. I know we both agreed that this is

> *The days got shorter, and the nights grew colder. It soon began to snow, and the ground was covered by a shimmering white blanket.*

where we would stay, and we would take our chances because it provided the best chance to remain undetected. But I think things have changed, and we need to consider other options. What do you think?"

Casey did not respond for a few moments as he gathered his thoughts. He hated the thought of changing their plans and exposing themselves to a greater risk of detection, but as he saw the concern in Taylor's eyes and the touch of fear in her voice, he had to admit that they probably needed to seek more permanent shelter.

He finally answered her question. "I've been thinking about this for some time also, and I agree we would probably be wise to move to a better location. I remember passing some cabins as we drove here. Maybe we can move to one of those. They will probably be unoccupied for the winter. We can stay there until spring and then move back up here. Does that sound better?"

Taylor gave him a big hug. "That sounds wonderful, but do you think we will be okay."

Casey squeezed her as tight as he dared. "I think we have to take the chance. I'll go down and try to locate one in the morning."

Dawn came. It was snowing. The next day it was still snowing. The third day it continued to snow, and when it finally stopped, the trail was covered with twelve to eighteen inches of fresh snow. They went to bed that night completely discouraged but prayed for God to make a way.

The next morning Casey got up with the sun and peered out the cabin door. To his amazement, half of the snow was gone. A warm wind blowing up the canyon had appeared in the night. It continued to blow all day, and by nightfall, the snow was almost gone. With buoyed spirits, he and Taylor knelt in prayer, thanking God for making a way.

The following morning, Casey put on his warm winter clothes and insulated hiking boots, kissed Taylor goodbye, and with a song in his heart and a promise to Taylor that he would be back by dark, headed down the trail. At times, the footing was slippery from melted snow, and in places, the stream was out of its banks, but he managed to clear the trail and, in a couple of hours, reach the bank of the river. The river was a little high, but he was still able to use the big boulders to make a safe crossing.

Once on the road, the going got easier. The challenge now was to find a cabin. About six miles down the road, he noticed a small opening in the line of trees bordering the road. As he got closer, he could see that it was an opening for a narrow road leading toward the river. He turned down the road, and after a short distance, he saw a cabin.

Casey approached the front door. It was locked. He went around to the back and located another door, which appeared to be to the kitchen. It, too, was locked. Not to be discouraged, he returned to the front door and searched for a key.

He knew that most cabin owners left a key somewhere because it was the unwritten rule of the mountains to make it easy to get into the cabins in an emergency. But there was no key under the mat or on top of the door sill. There was an outside light beside the door, and upon taking a closer look, he found a key on top of the light.

He explored the cabin. It appeared that no one had been there for some time. The kitchen was well-stocked with food, and there was a good supply of wood for the living room fireplace and the wood stove in the kitchen. There were several kerosene lamps throughout the house, and he located an additional supply of kerosene in the closet of the mudroom. *Perfect*, he thought to himself. *This will do nicely for the winter*. With a new sense of well-being, he locked the door behind him and headed back to the road.

Casey's heart was happy, and his steps light as he made his way up the road. However, his heart sank as he arrived at the crossing to the canyon trail. Where that morning he had crossed the South Fork of the Boise River by stepping from boulder to boulder, there was only madly rushing water. The melting snow from the higher elevations had finally made it down the river. He debated whether to return to the cabin, spend the night, and try again in the morning or chance a crossing through the tumbling, rushing water today. His concern was for Taylor. There was no way to get in touch with her, and he knew if he did not show up today, she would be distraught with fear and concern. Finally, he concluded that he had no choice. He had to try to get across and return to Taylor today.

He waded into the rushing water. The torrent swirled around his boots. So far, so good. But as he waded into the deeper water, he lost his footing and fell into the rushing water. It swept him headlong downstream, turning him from side to side.

He felt a sharp pain in his side as the water crushed him against a submerged boulder. He had to fight to keep his head above water. After what seemed like an eternity, he felt a force thrust him toward the opposite bank, where he grabbed an exposed tree root. He was able to plant his feet on solid ground, and with much effort, pull himself up on the bank.

He lay there for a few moments to catch his breath. He was alive with only a few bruises. The pain in his side had eased. But he was sopping wet. He had to get to the cabin as quickly as possible and change into some dry clothes. Otherwise, he might catch a bad cold or worse, pneumonia, or even worse, freeze to death.

Casey moved back upstream to where the trail headed up the valley and began his climb up to the cabin. Halfway up the valley, he started to shiver and feel weak, but he kept on climbing. When he reached the cabin, he was shivering so hard he couldn't stop.

Taylor greeted him as he entered the door. "Casey, what happened to you? You look a mess, and your clothes are sopping wet."

Casey was too cold to speak as he quickly but with great difficulty shed his wet clothes.

Taylor grabbed his arm and pushed him toward the bed. "Casey, get under the covers."

Casey obliged, and she joined him, moving close and wrapping her arms around him. He continued to shiver, but her body heat and the bedcovers gave him warmth, and the shivering subsided. He was finally able to speak, and he told her of his fall into the river and the mysterious force that had pushed him to the bank and probably saved his life.

"I found a cabin that will be just what we need to survive the winter and provide a warm place for our new baby, but we may have to wait a few days before we can move so we can safely get across the river."

They remained under the covers for the rest of that day and night. Casey woke up the next morning with a headache, runny nose, and a terrible cough. But he got out of bed and started to put on his remaining dry winter clothes.

"I'll go down and check the river."

"Casey, you sound terrible. You get back in bed. I'll go down and check the river. Besides, it's a nice day, and I need the exercise."

Casey mildly protested, but with a grin, climbed back into bed as he began another coughing spell.

Between fixing the daily meals and some herbal tea from their stock of wild plants, Taylor made two trips to the river. Upon return, each time she reported that the river was still very high, and as far as she could tell, impassable. She repeated the routine the next day with the same report.

On the third day, upon return from her morning trip, she reported that the river seemed to be back to normal, and the boulders that they had used to cross that summer were clearly visible.

The three days of rest and the herbal tea seemed to have worked miracles on Casey's cold, and he felt good enough to begin moving them to the vacant cabin. Fortunately, the cold did not progress to pneumonia, and he felt ready and strong. Taylor also seemed ready to make the move, refreshed from the three days of exercise she got from making the trips to the river.

They filled their backpacks with as much as they could carry and headed down the valley. When they got to the river, they found it as Taylor had reported, so they easily crossed over to the road. As they walked along the road, they felt a sense of well-being and began to express their joy with a song. The six miles sped by rapidly as they sang all the way to the front door of the vacant cabin.

Casey retrieved the key, unlocked the door, and motioned for Taylor to enter. "Welcome to your new home, sweetheart! It's the best I could do!"

Taylor walked around touching the furniture, admiring the fireplace, the kitchen, and the big comfortable bed. "Casey, I love it! But, but do you think we will be okay here? What if the owners come back?"

He enfolded her in his arms and gave her a kiss on the forehead. "I think we will be okay for the winter. From the pictures around, it looks like they were primarily here in the summer. Of course, come spring, we will have to move back up the valley. This will be a better place for the baby to come, so I think we need to take our chances and hope for the best. God has taken good care of us so far, and we must rely on Him to see us through."

Over the next few days, Casey made several more trips to their campsite to bring down the rest of their supplies that included their very important birth kit. Taylor stayed busy putting her personal touches on their new winter home.

Chapter 18
The Birth

After only a few days, they had become very familiar and comfortable in their "new" home. Casey kept a warm fire going in the fireplace and had managed to scrounge around and find enough firewood to replenish the cabin owner's supply. Taylor was quick to learn where things were in the kitchen and appreciated the well-stocked pantry. With only a month to go before the expected birth, she wanted to make sure all would be ready when the time came.

With less and less to do each day, they turned their attention to reading the guide to midwifery book that Casey had purchased. They read it and reread it several times to make sure they were prepared when it was time.

Each day, Taylor also checked and rechecked the items they had brought in the birth kit. She made sure that the kit still contained medical gloves, rubbing alcohol, hydrogen peroxide, a pair of scissors, a sharp knife, a baby blanket, a bulb syringe, Tylenol, a thermometer, olive oil, suture supplies, hand sanitizer, shoelaces, a cold compress, and trash bags. Some of these items were duplicates of what was in the cabin, but they had not anticipated the luxury the cabin offered. However, they didn't plan to use any of the cabin's supplies unless absolutely necessary. Not only did they consider it wrong, but any missing items might alert the owners of their use of the cabin.

In late November, Taylor was standing in front of the kitchen sink, finishing washing the breakfast dishes when the first one hit. It was a sharp cramp that lasted about thirty seconds. Casey was still sitting at the kitchen table, finishing his cup of herbal tea. She finished the dishes and returned to sit beside him. About twenty minutes later, she had another contraction.

"Casey, I think the time has come. I just had a second contraction, and I think we had better get things ready. I don't know how long it will take. The book says from ten to twenty hours, but I think we need to be prepared."

They laid out the items from the birth kit, checking each one to make sure they were still useful. They stripped the bed and replaced the bottom sheet with a plastic tablecloth they found in the kitchen. Casey brought fresh water from the river and started heating a big pot of water on the kitchen stove.

For the next couple hours, they checked the time interval between contractions, but then gave that up and only checked once every hour. They first tried to move around the house, cleaning here and tidying there, but that became useless, so they tried reading. Neither activity seemed to keep their minds off the anticipation of the next contraction. As the day wore on, the pains became more intense, and the interval between pains less and less until by twelve hours from the first pain, they were coming every two to three minutes.

The next three hours were a living torture. Taylor pushed, she cried, she moaned, she even screamed a few times as the baby emerged. Casey could only stand by, hold her hand, and keep a cool cloth on her forehead. The delivery appeared to go according to the book. Casey followed the book's instructions as it became his time to clamp and cut the cord and clean Taylor and the baby. Fortunately, Taylor did not tear during the delivery, so Casey did not have to use the sutures in the birth kit.

> *If it was a boy, they had decided to name him John after John the Baptist. They jokingly said that their John would probably also be one "crying in the wilderness"*

It was a boy. If it was a boy, they had decided to name him John after John the Baptist. They jokingly said that their John would probably also be one "crying in the wilderness" (see John 1:23).

Casey completed the final cleanup and placed John in the arms of Taylor. He had a new love and appreciation for his wife as he gazed fondly at the mother and son lying on the bed so peacefully. The ordeal was finally over, and he looked forward to being a father and a better husband. Taylor smiled weakly, drew the baby tightly to her, and closed her eyes.

Casey placed the bloody remnants from the birth in a plastic bag, took them outside, and buried them in a hole he had dug when they had first arrived at the cabin. He returned to the cabin and found Taylor and John still asleep. He pulled up a chair beside the bed, took hold of Taylor's free hand, laid his head on the bed, and was soon fast asleep.

A storm was blowing in, and the wind howled around the cabin. Soon the snow started, and the darkness deepened. However, the cabin was warm and secure, sufficient protection for the little family seeking shelter from the storms of life.

Chapter 19
Is God Still There?

It was mid-morning. The wind and snow had stopped, and the sun was shining. The new-fallen snow glistened in the sunlight. Casey was still asleep in the chair beside the bed when his subconscious was disturbed by an unfamiliar sound, a baby crying. He lifted his groggy head from the bed and realized that the sound was coming from John lying in the crook of Taylor's arm. He still was half asleep, but he sensed that something was terribly wrong. Taylor's hand was cold. He squeezed it ever so gently, but there was no response.

He became quickly alert.

"Taylor, wake up. I think John may be hungry."

There was no response. Casey rose from the chair and moved closer to the bed. He felt of Taylor's forehead. It was as cold as her hand. Now he was really alarmed.

"Taylor, please, please wake up," he pleaded as a tear began to run down his cheek.

He grabbed her wrist and felt for a pulse. There was none. He tried CPR, but there was still no response. Then he noticed the large pool of blood on the tablecloth that she had been lying on.

Now frantic, he pleaded. "Taylor, please, sweetheart, you can't do this to us. We desperately need you; John needs you; I need you. How will we ever make it without you?"

But he knew she was dead. Casey knelt beside the still body and cast his eyes toward heaven.

"God, please don't take her now. What are we going to do without her? Please bring her back to us. Little John especially needs her. I can survive, but he desperately needs her. I still trust You, though, and know that You will make a way for us. Just give me the strength to get us through this."

Casey was interrupted by a louder cry from John, so he arose from his knees and gently took John from Taylor's lifeless arm, wrapped him in a warm blanket, and headed for the kitchen. He prepared one of the packets of dried baby formula that they had brought with them for emergencies, and John soon had devoured most of the bottle. Casey changed his diaper, wrapped him in his blanket, and placed him on the small couch in the bedroom.

He returned to the bed and stared down at Taylor's lifeless body. He still had trouble believing that she was gone. But seeing her lying there, he knew that she was and that he and John now faced some real challenges.

The first challenge would be where to bury Taylor. He couldn't bury her here. The ground would be too frozen to even try to dig a grave deep enough. He would have to take her body back to the cabin at Heart Lake. Maybe he could dig a grave in their cabin. Maybe the ground would not be as frozen since it had been dry. Yes, that was what he had to do. The challenge would be getting her body to the cabin while also carrying John.

The second challenge would be food for John. They only had about a two-week supply of the emergency powdered formula, and that was certainly not long enough for John to be able to take and digest regular food. He would have to find another source of milk, but where in this isolated location and in the depth of winter.

The challenges seemed to be too much, and Casey began to doubt that he could meet them. His thoughts went round and round in his brain. *Maybe I should give it all up and return to Buhl. Maybe the government will be lenient because of the circumstances. Maybe it would be best for John to become a ward of the State. Maybe I should give up and face the consequences. But I can't. I have no way of getting in touch with anyone to come and get us. The bridges were burned when we left Buhl.*

Casey once more looked at Taylor's lifeless body and John sleeping quietly in his bed. "No, I am not going to give up my son. I am going to see this through, no matter what it takes. I still believe there is a loving God, and He will provide!"

With a new burst of determination and resolve, Casey retreated to the couch in front of the fireplace and began to plan the trip up to the Heart Lake cabin.

That afternoon, he zipped Taylor's lifeless body in a sleeping bag and attached a rope to the front flap that would go around his waist and allow him to pull her up the road and the trail to the cabin. Of course, he would have to also take John with him, but that would not be a problem because Taylor had the foresight to bring a baby pouch that would allow Casey to carry John strapped to his chest. It would be hard, but with good weather, they should be able to complete the round trip and bury Taylor in one long day.

Casey also disposed of the bloody tablecloth and returned the bedroom to its clean and tidy condition. After feeding John another bottle of the formula, he went to bed, praying that tomorrow would bring good weather.

Chapter 20
The Burial

Casey had a rather sleepless night. John was up and down most of the night and seemed to be only comforted if he was held and rocked. He was glad when morning came, and he could get on with his plan for Taylor. He fed John his morning bottle and prepared two more bottles to take with them. Casey was relieved that the day was clear and bright.

> *Casey carried the sleeping bag containing Taylor's lifeless body to the front porch and lowered it onto the ground.*

Casey dressed John in warm clothes and loaded him in the chest pouch. John seemed to find comfort in being bundled up and close and fell fast asleep. Casey carried the sleeping bag containing Taylor's lifeless body to the front porch and lowered it onto the ground. He wound the rope around his waist, secured it with a bowline knot, and headed up the road.

When he reached the main road, he paused to catch his breath and survey the condition of the road. Fortunately, the high winds of the previous storm had blown most of the snow off the road and into snowbanks on the side of the road.

He thought to himself, *This may not be that bad. I'll just take my time and save my energy for the trail up the valley.*

With that thought, he headed up the road. He felt bad that Taylor had to be transported this way with her lifeless body feeling every bump in the road, but there was no other way. It seemed that it took forever to travel the six miles to the end of the road because he had to stop and rest often, but they finally arrived. Now the challenge would be to get across the river. He would have to carry the body across the river, stepping from rock to rock and hope he would not slip and fall into the icy river. If that happened, he would be alright, but John would get wet, and Casey was sure that would spell disaster.

Casey lifted the lifeless body up onto his shoulders and wrapped his arms around her neck and legs. The exertion apparently disturbed John, and he let out a whimper.

Oh great! thought Casey. *This would be a very bad time for John to wake up and move around in the chest pouch.*

Casey stood on the riverbank for a few minutes, and John settled back into his pouch.

Casey stepped on the first rock, then the second, and the third. He was in the middle of the river when Taylor's body shifted, and he almost lost his balance. But with all of his strength, he adjusted her body and gained his footing. With relief, he stepped on the last rock and then the river bank.

He gently lowered Taylor's body to the ground and stood there for several minutes as he caught his breath and said a short prayer, thanking God for helping him with a most difficult task.

After catching his breath, he returned to the other riverbank and got the sleeping bag. Crossing the river again, he marveled at how John had slept through all that. He placed Taylor's body back in the sleeping bag, reattached the rope around his waist, checked on John, and headed up the valley trail.

The trip up the main road was a picnic compared to what the trail offered. It was covered with snow, sometimes almost up to his knees. Each step was agony, but he kept pushing on. After what seemed like an eternity, they finally reached the cabin. A snowdrift blocked the door, and the roof was covered with a deep blanket of snow, but it was still standing.

He untied the rope around his waist, secured the sleeping bag containing Taylor's lifeless body to a nearby tree, and began removing the snowdrift from the door. All he had to use was a small tree branch, so it took him several minutes to remove it, but finally, he could move the door enough for him to enter. The interior of the cabin was as they had left it weeks earlier.

He removed John from the chest pouch and laid him on the bed. John stirred but remained asleep. There was still a pile of wood against the wall, and Casey debated whether to start a big fire and dispose of the body by burning, but thought better. A large fire might attract someone and might not fully cremate the body. No, the only thing he could do was dig a grave. He removed the floorboards and tested the dirt floor of the cabin, and as he had hoped, it was not frozen. He grabbed the shovel they had left at the cabin and started to dig.

Casey had barely scratched the surface when John began to cry, so he had to stop and see what he needed. Really not knowing what to do, he resorted to the obvious and offered John one of the bottles he had brought with him. He had no way to heat it, but it had been carried in one of the inside pockets of his jacket, so the formula was near body temperature. It seemed to work, and soon John was back to sleep. Casey resumed digging.

The digging was not easy, but after a couple of hours, he had fashioned a trench about two feet wide, six feet long and four feet deep. He stared at the trench for a few minutes, dreading what he had to do next but knew it had to be done. He carried the sleeping bag containing the lifeless body into the cabin and slowly lowered it into the trench. Tears flowed down his cheeks as he gazed at the makeshift grave. Through the sobs he offered a simple prayer.

"God, I have just placed the love of my life into the ground. I have faith that You will watch over her and someday soon, raise her to be with You forever. Please give me the faith and the strength to remain true to You so we can be together again. Help me also to do all I can to take care of John so we can be a family again. Amen"

Still sobbing, Casey reluctantly began shoveling the dirt back into the trench. He replaced the floor timbers, leaned the shovel against the wall, placed the sleeping John back in the chest pouch, gazed once again at the spot where his love lay, and exited the cabin. One challenge was met and completed, but he still had another big one to solve. Where was he going to get the proper food for John?

With John snugly in the chest pouch, Casey headed down the valley, hoping to get back to the vacant cabin before dark. It was a lot easier going as they descended down the valley, and there was no problem crossing the river. Soon they were back at the vacant cabin; John was fed again and put to bed.

Then it hit. Casey fully realized that Taylor was no longer there, and he once again felt the tears stream down his face. It was a lonely feeling, and he was not sure that he would ever be the same. His only hope was his faith in God. He had to hold on to that no matter what happened. With that, he collapsed into bed and was soon deep in sleep.

Chapter 21
The Answer

    John fussed several times during the night, so Casey did not have the rest he thought he needed. However, after the last feeding, John settled down, and Casey was able to get three hours of deep sleep before John woke up again. It was dawn anyway, so Casey got up, fixed a bottle, changed, and fed John. While he was feeding John, he felt impressed to get out of the cabin and go for a walk. But why? He had more than enough exercise the previous day to last a week. Nevertheless, after making his bed and cleaning John and the kitchen, he put on his winter hiking clothes, dressed John in warm clothes, tucked him in the chest pouch, and headed out the door.
    When he got to the main road, he hesitated. "Which way should I go, left or right?" He looked to the left and thought to himself, *I went that way yesterday. I think I'll go right this time.*
    He had walked probably two miles when he spotted something moving in a snowdrift on the side of the road. It appeared to be an animal of some kind, so he slowly and cautiously moved toward it. As he got closer, he could see that what looked like a goat was stuck in the snowdrift and was frantically trying to get free.
    As he got even closer, he could see that it was a goat, so he tried to calm it down by quietly talking.

"Hey, little fellow, where did you come from? Be still, and I'll try to get you out of that drift. Calm down; it's going to be all right."

The goat began to settle down as Casey reached and stroked its head.

Keeping one hand busy patting the goat's head, Casey was able to get the other hand under its stomach and gently lift it high enough out of the snow for the goat to finish freeing itself. It shook to remove the remaining snow caked to its skin and bleated, "Naaaaaaaa," as if to say, "Thank you!"

At that moment, Casey realized that he had probably just saved the life of a nanny goat. Nanny goats produce milk. Goat's milk is as close to mother's milk as anything. Maybe, just maybe, here is the answer to our second challenge, a sustainable food supply for John.

The problem was now how to get Nanny to the cabin and keep her around. Once he got her there, he might be able to tether her with a rope, but he could not carry her there with John strapped to his chest. What if she gave a sudden kick and hit John in the head? No, he would have to figure another way to get Nanny to the cabin.

He studied Nanny for a moment. She stared back with her head cocked to one side as if to say, "What's the problem?"

Casey took a risk, turned, and started back up the road toward the cabin. He knew that some domesticated animals would instinctively follow a human and hoped that Nanny would follow her instincts. He had only taken a few steps when he felt Nanny by his side, and the two of them were soon at the cabin.

John seemed to thrive on Nanny's milk and, much to Casey's relief was soon sleeping through the night.

Nanny adjusted well to being with Casey and John. She stayed in the cabin with them, and when she felt the need to go outside, Casey found her at the cabin's back door. She always came back. There was no animal food in the house, so somehow, on her excursions, she evidently found enough food to sustain her. She always stood still when Casey milked her and always gave enough milk to sustain John each day. John seemed to thrive on Nanny's milk and, much to Casey's relief was soon sleeping through the night. Nanny became a dear part of the family. Casey, over and over, thanked God for providing a way.

Winter's icy grasp soon gave way to warmer days. The snows along the road and river melted, and the meadows began to blossom with flowers and grasses. Casey hated to leave the comforts of the cabin but knew each day there was an increasing risk that they might be discovered. He had heard an occasional vehicle on the main road, probably someone from the forest service.

The time had come to move back up the valley. He tried to return everything in the cabin to the way he and Taylor had found it but knew he probably missed something. He would have to hope that when the owners returned, they would not be that perceptive.

He had already made a few trips up the valley, taking their supplies back to the cabin. It had withstood the winter well and would be sufficient for another summer. It was now time for the last trip. He strapped John to his chest, donned his backpack with the last of their possessions, locked the cabin for the last time, and the three of them, Casey, John, and Nanny headed for the main road.

Chapter 22

Sunday Law

Sheriff Scott took a break, grabbed a cup of coffee, returned to his desk, and opened his computer to today's *New York Times*. After glancing at the headlines, which at the moment did not interest him, he turned to the second page. One headline caught his eye. It was titled:

"*Supreme Court Upholds New Sunday Law*"

Always interested in court decisions that might affect how he operated the sheriff's department, he began to read.

The unthinkable has happened. In less than a year, religious intolerance has gained control in the United States. It had been confidently believed that the United States could never become anything but the defender of religious liberty. For many years, the issue of enforcing the observance of Sunday as the official day of Christian worship had been debated but never been seriously considered by Congress.

However, in the interest of unity and the welfare of the U.S. citizens in these troubled times, church leaders, Congress, and the president have combined to pass a law declaring Sunday as a national day of rest. No businesses can be open on Sunday. No sporting events, theaters, amusement parks, or any secular activity are allowed on Sunday. All people in the United States, regardless of religious beliefs otherwise, must spend that day in worship and family fellowship.

A small minority that chooses to worship God on Saturday, the Sabbath, the true day of worship as commanded in the Ten Commandments, quickly appealed, declaring that the law was unconstitutional. The Supreme Court just as quickly declared the law to be constitutional and the law of the land.

The Sabbath is now a test of loyalty, the final test, drawing the line of distinction between those who serve God and those who serve man. The compliance with the new state-mandated religious Sunday law is now a sign of allegiance to the power of the State. Observance of the Ten-Commandment Sabbath as the declared obedience of God's law and recognition of His creative power is no longer permitted.

The small minority, however, have refused to accept the new law. The religious and secular leaders have declared that those few who stand in the way of the new law should not be tolerated and that it is better for them to be exterminated than for the whole nation to suffer from their disobedience. It is expected that a final executive order will be issued, declaring that those who persist in observing the Sabbath of the fourth commandment deserve the severest punishment, even death. The plan is for a final solution.

Sheriff Scott could not believe what he had just read. He had not received a copy of the law and executive order and would have to read it before taking any action. However, he vowed that he would not let this happen in Twin Falls County. He would not allow vigilante groups to harm or kill anyone who observed the Sabbath, even if it meant the loss of his job. He felt strongly that the US Constitution protected the religious minorities, and as long as he could, he and his staff would do their best to protect their right to worship whenever they so chose. He hoped that the other law enforcement officers in the state would feel the same.

He recalled that when they were attempting to find information about the disappearance of Casey and Taylor Denney that Harry had contacted the pastor of the Twin Falls SDA church and some of the Denneys' friends. Maybe he would take his staff to that church this Saturday and provide a presence to guard against any attempt of violence to the congregation.

Sheriff Scott called his deputies into his office and announced, "I want all four of us to meet at the Twin Falls SDA Church about nine o'clock Saturday morning just to be sure there isn't any trouble because of this new Sunday law."

Harry was curious. "Sunday law? What's that all about?"

The sheriff suggested, "Check out the second page of today's *New York Times*.

Harry nodded and left to clear his calendar and see what was in the *New York Times*.

Chapter 23

Saturday Morning

A few minutes before 9:00 o' Saturday morning, Sheriff Scott drove into the parking lot of the Twin Falls SDA Church. There were only three other cars in the parking lot, and no one was in sight. He parked his cruiser near the entrance of the parking lot, shut off his engine, and rolled down the driver and passenger-side windows.

It was a mild and pleasant morning with no hint of what threatening clouds might be forming in the world. Sheriff Scott expected to be in the cruiser for a few hours and did not want it to overheat. Besides, he had persuaded his wife, Sherri, to join him, and he for sure wanted her to be comfortable.

A few minutes later, Harry pulled into the parking lot and stopped by to say hello to the sheriff. "Where do you want me to park?"

"Pick any spot in the southeast corner. I see you brought the family with you?"

"Yeah! I showed her the article from the *New York Times,* and she insisted. She wants to see what all this fuss was about the Sabbath. Mrs. Scott, would you like to join her?"

"Sure, but let's wait until a few more people show up."

"Good idea. Just come on over when you think the time is right."

Harry parked in the suggested area, and soon Tom and Phil showed up. Sheriff Scott directed them to the northeast and northwest corners of the parking lot.

Between 9:00 and 9:30, more people began to arrive, and then from 9:30 to 11:00, the parking lot filled up rapidly. Sheriff Scott could tell by their body language and subdued talk that most arrived with what he guessed was a deep concern of what the future would hold. But they still greeted each other with a smile, a hug, and even a few exchanges of "Happy Sabbath" as they poured into the church.

Ray and LeAnn King and their neighbors, Barbara and Mark Wehtje, arrived and greeted some of their neighbors that they had invited to worship with them. The neighbors had been impressed at the friendliness and caring that the two couples had shown them and were eager to find out more about the church that met on Saturday.

Blair and Megan arrived shortly thereafter and welcomed some of the people that worked with him at the bank. The bank people had been impressed with Blair's kindness and fairness in dealing with the bank employees. They were curious to learn if it had something to do with his and Megan's commitment to Christ and the Sabbath.

Ashley and Kevin drifted in next, and they, too, welcomed some of Ashley's restaurant employees that had been waiting for them. They had gladly accepted the invitation to join Ashley and Kevin at church because they, too, were curious about what prompted Ashley to close her restaurant every Saturday, which was usually the busiest time for most restaurants. They were also concerned for the future of the restaurant and their jobs if Ashley had to stay closed on Sunday also. Kevin's drug store had managed to survive and prosper even though he only kept the pharmacy part of the store open for business on Saturday and Sunday.

Sara and Joe, with their two daughters, were next to arrive. They were joined by some of the employees at the R&D facility who had a great deal of respect for Joe and were curious if the Sabbath was in any way responsible for his caring personality.

Last to arrive were Jake and Christie and Alisha, who boldly had also invited some friends to join them for the worship service. They found those friends seated on the back rows, awaiting their arrival.

Sheriff Scott saw his wife Sherri and Harry's wife and daughter enter the church and decided to join them. As he entered the church, he was greeted with a warm welcome from who he assumed were some of the church members, handed a bulletin, and ushered to a seat in the balcony. There were no seats left on the main floor. The sanctuary was packed. He recognized the mayor, the chief of police, and most of the city council. He was amazed to also see Sam and her husband in the second row. He had not asked her to attend, but there she was.

> *The sanctuary was packed. He recognized the mayor, the chief of police, and most of the city council.*

The service went by quickly, the music was good, the prayers seemed to be sincere, and the pastor gave an excellent Christ-centered sermon that connected the observance of the seventh-day Sabbath to Christ as the Creator and soon-returning Savior.

Sheriff Scott met his wife at his cruiser. Without a word, they stood by the cruiser and watched the people leave. Some still had that look of concern, but most left with a smile and body language that seemed to say, "Jesus, if it's time for Your return, then so be it!"

After all had left, the pastor approached them and expressed his thanks to them for coming to the service. "Sheriff, I am Pastor Kaufman. We appreciated you and your men showing a police presence, but what prompted you to be here today?"

Sheriff Scott looked at Harry as if to say. "Do you want to answer that?" Harry mouthed a reply, "You go ahead!"

Sheriff Scott turned back to face the pastor. "It's probably nothing, but this last week there were a lot of comments on social media about how the Seventh-day Adventists were not honoring the new Sunday Law and what should be done about it! Frankly, some of the comments and threats were alarming, and we just thought we should come by today to make sure you and your people were not harmed. But what is so important about having your services on Saturday and not going along with the new Sunday Law? I don't understand!"

Sensing an opportunity to witness and recognizing that the Sheriff was sincere in asking the question, the pastor responded. "First, let me make sure you understand that we believe that there is a heaven and an eternity ruled by God and that we are saved for eternity by believing in God's Son, Jesus, and by His loving sacrifice on the cross of Calvary. Because of that sacrifice and His love, we ask, what would You have us to do. Jesus responded to that question by saying–"If you love Me, keep My commandments," which to us includes the Ten Commandments. Sheriff, I am sure you agree we would have a better world if everyone obeyed all of the Ten Commandments, especially the ones about murder, lying, telling the truth, adultery, honoring authority, and stealing.

Sheriff Scott agreed. "Yes, that would make our job a lot easier and maybe even put us out of a job."

The pastor continued. "To us, all ten of the commandments are important, and that includes the fourth commandment, remember to keep the Sabbath day holy. It is important because it is the only commandment that tells us who God is, what is His realm, and what is His power. He is the Creator and Ruler of the universe, and He has the power to create a new heart in us. Do you realize that there is no astrological reason for a seven-day week? It was created by God, and He rested on the seventh day."

"But how do you know that today is the Sabbath, the seventh day?"

"Look at a calendar—what day is the seventh day?"

"Saturday."

"Right, and what do they call Sunday?"

"The first day of the week?"

"The real clincher, according to history and the Bible, is that Jesus rested in the tomb on Sabbath and was resurrected on the first day of the week, universally agreed to be Sunday.

"But wouldn't God be okay with resting on any day of the week. That way, you would not be in violation of the new Sunday law?"

"The fourth commandment specifically says to remember **the** Sabbath day; it does not say remember **a** Sabbath day. So it comes down to who do you honor, God's law or man's law. Do you now understand why we honor and keep Saturday as our day of worship?"

"Yes, and I appreciate you taking the time to explain."

"Do you have any more questions?"

Harry and the sheriff looked at each other and shook their heads no.

"If not, then, thanks again for coming by today. I think we will be alright and not have too much trouble continuing to worship on Saturday. After all, the people in Twin Falls are law-abiding citizens and would not cause any trouble. But you and your deputies are more than welcome to join us on Sabbath if you can. We would enjoy having you. I need to go lock up and take my family home for a good Sabbath meal. God bless!!"

On the drive home, Sheriff Scott broke the silence. "That was something. I had no idea what they believed or why they placed so much emphasis on Saturday as the Sabbath blessed by God. I think I understand a little, and I would like to come back next week to learn more. Sherri, how do you feel?"

"I would like to learn more too!"

"Well, next week, we will give it a try unless there is a crisis or emergency that I need to take care of. But, I see no need to have all four of us here unless they also want to attend the services.

Chapter 24
A Lead

Sam picked up the phone. "Hello, Twin Falls County Sheriff. How may I help you?"

She listened for a few minutes and replied, "One moment, please, and I will connect you to Sheriff Scott."

Sam buzzed Sheriff Scott. "It's Sheriff Sandy David from the Camas County Sheriff's Office."

Sheriff Scott picked up his phone. "Hello. This is Sheriff Scott. What can I do for you, Sandy?"

Sheriff Scott had known Sandy for many years through their involvement in the Idaho Sheriff's Association, so he listened intently and responded. "Thanks for the information. I agree it's a possibility. Would it be okay for a couple of us to join you in the investigation?"

Sheriff Scott was pleased with the response. They chatted for a few more minutes and closed the conversation.

After hanging up the phone, Sheriff Scott buzzed Harry. "Harry, join me in my office. We may have a lead on the missing Denney couple."

Harry took a seat, and the sheriff relayed the information he had received from Sheriff David. "I just got a call from Camas County Sheriff Sandy David. He got a call from an owner of a cabin on the South Fork of the Boise River. The owners are from Boise, and they were at the cabin over the weekend getting it ready for the summer season. They noticed that a few things in the cabin were not the way they had left them last fall and suspected that someone had broken in and maybe stayed during the winter."

The sheriff continued. "They brought their dog with them, and it seems the dog located a shallow hole that contained a number of items related to the birth of a child. Sheriff David and one of his deputies are going up there next week to check things and said it would be alright if we joined them."

"I'll call the FBI and see if they are interested in joining us also. So, clear your calendar for next week. We'll head up there on Monday.

Sheriff Scott buzzed Sam. "Sam, get me the FBI office in Boise."

Sam obliged, and soon Sheriff Scott was on the line with the FBI agent, explaining the report and the purpose of their trip to Camas County.

After he hung up, he buzzed Harry again and announced. "Harry, the FBI agent said they were very busy now and could not join us next week but to keep them informed of any new developments. It's just you and me and the Camas County people."

Chapter 25
The Search

Sheriff Scott and Harry met early Monday morning at the sheriff's office. Sheriff Scott was standing beside a trailer that was hooked to the department's SUV and was loaded with the department's two ATVs. Sheriff Scott piled into the driver's side, and Harry assumed the shotgun position. An hour and a half later they pulled into the Camas County Sheriff's Office parking lot.

Sheriff David was waiting for them and invited them into his office. "Can I interest you in some coffee?"

Both Sheriff Scott and Harry gladly accepted the offer. Between sips Sheriff Scott asked if there had been anything new happen since they last spoke.

Sheriff David cleared his throat and responded. "Yes, there has been. We sent the items found by the dog to the lab in Boise, and they were definitely things from a childbirth. We are waiting on the analysis of the blood found on the tablecloth for information about DNA and blood type. We

We are waiting on the analysis of the blood found on the tablecloth for information about DNA and blood type.

searched the area around the cabin but found no other evidence or clues about who might have stayed in the cabin."

Offering another cup of coffee that was gladly accepted, Sheriff David continued. "I suggest we expand our search today to see if we can find anything else that might answer our questions. We have ATVs also, and we have permission from the U.S. Forest Service to go off-road if we think it's necessary. I've also got a pair of bloodhounds that we can use. One of my deputies will go with us to handle the dogs. We can stop at the cabin and see if they can pick up any scent of who stayed there. If they are still in the area, the dogs should be able to track them."

After a quick trip to the restroom, the four officers met in the parking lot and got into their vehicles. Sheriff David was driving a Dodge Ram crew cab pickup with a shell to give the bloodhounds a safe place to ride. Ninety minutes later they pulled into the cabin driveway. They inspected the inside and outside of the cabin for possible clues but did not find anything that would help. They let the bloodhounds search inside and out to see if they could pick up a scent and then got back in their vehicles. Sheriff Scott asked, "Where do we start?"

Sheriff David suggested, "The road continues for five or six miles. Let's drive up there and see if we find anything."

They parked the vehicles at the end of the road, and when they let the dogs out, they quickly went to the riverbank and began sniffing around. Sheriff David watched the two dogs move up and down the river bank, turned to Sheriff Scott and announced that he thought the dogs had picked up a scent but weren't sure where it went. He suggested that they take the ATVs on up the river to see if the dogs could find a trail. They unloaded the ATVs, climbed on board, and started the engines.

Casey was outside the cabin when he heard the dogs bark and the engines roar. He listened quietly as the sound of the engines faded into the distance. Probably some ATV riders out for a test drive of their new machines, but he felt like he needed to take a closer look. He checked on eight-month-old John. He was sound asleep, having not been disturbed by the sudden roar of the engines. He would not need to be fed for three more hours, so he felt comfortable leaving him asleep to check on the visitors.

Casey headed down the trail. He kept hidden in the trees as much as he could as he made his way toward the river. He reached the edge of the forest just above the river and carefully peaked around a big pine tree. There was no sign of life.

The first vehicle he saw had *"Camas County Sheriff"* on the door. He thought, *Nothing unusual about the Camas County Sheriff being here. It's his jurisdiction. They are probably making a routine run through the area to make sure everything is okay after the winter.*

Then his heart sank as he read the logo on the side of the other vehicle. It read *"Twin Falls County Sheriff."*

"There can be only one reason for the Twin Falls County Sheriff to be in Camas County. They are looking for us! I must have overlooked something at the vacant cabin that alerted the Camas County Sheriff, and he contacted Twin Falls County Sheriff. Maybe the Twin Falls County Sheriff sent out something that the Camas County Sheriff saw and suspected that we were in the vicinity," he muttered to himself. "Who knows ? What matters is that they are here, and so are we."

Casey quickly retraced his steps back to the cabin. He checked on John. He was awake, so he picked him up and came outside. He held John tightly as he heard the ATV engines, first faintly in the distance, and then louder and louder as they came down the river. Then the engines stopped and silence filled the forest. A particular Bible text came to mind.

"Yes, I will trust the promises of God. And since I am trusting him, what can mere man do to me?" (Ps. 56:4, TLB).

Chapter 26
Discovery

"Stand firm and you will see the deliverance the Lord will bring you this day" (Exod. 14:13, NIV).

As Casey listened, he heard men yelling at the dogs, and soon the search party came into view climbing up the trail. There were two dogs and four men. It would not be long before they arrived at his campsite. He debated about what to do. He couldn't hide. He couldn't run. He had no intention of hurting the men or the dogs, even if he could. He and John were trapped. But he could pray!

"God, we need your help, and if it's not too much to ask, maybe one more miracle. Thank You for all the times You have helped us during this troubling time. I know we have not completely trusted You at all times, but You have seen fit to bless us and protect us anyway. We now, however, declare our trust in You and place our life and our future in Your hands. Save us! Amen!"

Still kneeling, he held John tightly to his chest. Tears ran down his cheeks as he gazed up to the heavens. His muscles tightened as he felt the two dogs come closer and take a position on his right and left, with bared teeth and menacing growls. He gently kissed John on the forehead and slowly stood.

As the four men approached, Sheriff David commanded the dogs to heel, and they stopped growling. He continued. "We're sorry to disturb you. I am Sandy David, Camas County Sheriff. This is my deputy, and these other two men are Sheriff Scott and his deputy, Harry. They are from Twin Falls County."

The four exchanged handshakes, and Sheriff David continued. "You have quite a set-up here. Does the Forest Service know about it?"

Casey hesitated and then offered a simple, "Not that I'm aware of!"

Sheriff David continued to press. "I see you have had a fire. Do you have a burn permit?

Again Casey offered a simple, "No!"

"We are looking for someone that may have occupied a cabin down the river this last winter. Do you know who that might be?"

Casey could not lie, so he confessed. "That was us!"

"What do you mean by us? Were there others also staying at the cabin?"

"Just three of us, my wife, the baby, and me."

"Where is your wife?"

Looking nervously at the two dogs, hoping that they would not pick up the scent of Taylor's body and not wanting to tell more than he had to, Casey merely said, "She's gone!"

The Camas County Sheriff pressed on. "She left you? When?"

"Right after John was born."

"Do you know where she went?"

"No!"

"You are not under arrest, but you need to come with us for further questioning."

"Let me get a few things for the baby, and I will go with you." As he moved into the cabin, his mind raced. *What if the dogs pick up a scent of the body. It's not buried very deep. I hate to leave here. The winter protected the grave, and I was going to prepare a deeper one as soon as weather permitted. What will they do to me? What will happen to John? What a mess! Why didn't I do a better job of removing any traces of our stay in the cabin? I wonder what tipped them off?*

His mind was still racing as he emerged from the cabin. Sheriff David motioned for him to join him as they started down the trail. The dogs ran ahead. Nanny emerged from behind the cabin where she had been hiding and joined the group.

Sheriff David stopped, looked at Nanny, and then at Casey. "A goat? Want to explain."

Casey proudly explained. "God provided her. One day at the cabin, I heard God speak to me. He told me to go for a walk. It was cold but sunny, so I bundled John up, put on my winter jacket, and we went for a walk. At the main road, God told me to go right. I did and found Nanny stuck in a snowdrift. I freed her. She has been our constant companion since and has been the source of milk for John. What is going to happen to her? I would hate to leave her here all alone."

Sheriff David responded, "We'll find a good home for her. Don't you worry."

With that, the party continued on down the trail. Sheriff Scott and Harry took up the rear. Sheriff Scott whispered to Harry. "Do you think this is Casey Denney?"

"I think so, but it's hard to tell. That beard covers a lot of his face, but if he's not, he's a close second."

"I guess we will find out once we get the chance to question him."

The party arrived at the vehicles. The ATVs were secured on the trailers, and the dogs were loaded into the SUVs. At the instruction of Sheriff David, Casey and Nanny piled into the rear seat of Sheriff Scott's vehicle. Casey remained silent as they made the trip to Fairfield, but his mind was at peace as he prayed.

> *Sheriff Scott whispered to Harry. "Do you think this is Casey Denney?"*

"Lord, thank You for dulling the senses of the dogs, so they did not discover Taylor's body. I know it is not the most ideal place for her to be right now, but I would appreciate it if You would send an angel to watch over her, keep her from wild animals, and preserve her for Your second coming. I hope to keep her location a secret, so give me the wisdom and words to make that happen. I don't know what is in store for me and John in the future, but we put our trust in You to guide us and comfort us. If it be Your will, I vow to return to Heart Lake someday to be with Taylor and want to be with her in heaven someday. Thanks for loving us and giving us strength!"

Chapter 27
Interrogation

Even though it was late in the afternoon, upon arrival in Fairfield, they went directly to the Camas County Sheriff's Office. Sheriff David had called ahead and arranged for a local rancher to meet them at the office and pick up the goat. Casey reluctantly handed her over to the rancher. "Please take good care of her. She was a gift from God, and she needs a good home."

The rancher, who had a kind but leathery face from many hours in the sun, picked up Nanny and shook Casey's hand. Casey had met several just like him, and like most of the ranchers in Southern Idaho, their word was their bond. If they made a promise, they were always good for it, so Casey was not surprised by the rancher's assurance. "Don't you worry, son, she will be just fine on the ranch. She seems real tame, so my kids will have a ball taking care of her. Are you sure you don't know who she belonged to? We could get her back to the owner if we had some idea where to look."

"I have no idea. I found her stuck in a snowbank up there on the South fork of the Boise River. Wherever she came from, I believe an angel planted her there just to help us out."

"Okay, I might ask a few friends about her, but in the meantime, I'll take good care of her." With that remark, the rancher loaded Nanny in his pickup, climbed into the driver's seat beside her, and drove off.

Sheriff David motioned toward the door of the building. "Let's all go inside!"

Sheriff David led the way, followed by Casey with John held tightly in his arms. Sheriff Scott and Harry entered last. They were met by the office receptionist, and Sheriff David explained to Casey. "This is Ilene, and I have asked her to take care of your baby while we get some information."

Casey hesitated and held John a little tighter.

"It's all right; we won't be gone long, and Ilene has two children of her own. She will take good care of the baby. Do you have a bottle just in case he might get hungry?"

Ilene approached Casey, stretched out her arms, looked reassuringly into Casey's eyes, and placed her hands under John. Casey let him go, but a tear appeared and moved slowly down his cheek. With a quiver in his voice, he managed to say, "There's a bottle of Nanny's milk in my backpack. He usually has no problem taking it. Also, there are a few cloth diapers."

Ilene nodded, and with John in her arms, moved toward the break room.

Sheriff David motioned to Casey, Sheriff Scott, and Harry to follow him, and they moved down the hall to what appeared to be a simple conference room, but in reality, it was an interrogation room complete with video-taping and a one-way window. All took a seat around a conference table. Sheriff David looked at Casey and broke the silence. "You have the right to remain silent. Anything you say can and will be used against you in a court of law. You have the right to an attorney. If you cannot afford an attorney, one will be provided for you."

Casey offered no response, and Sheriff David continued. "Care to give us your name?"

"Casey Denney."

Sheriff Scott and Harry exchanged swift glances, and each nodded their heads in recognition.

"Where's home?"

"Until last year, Buhl."

"Why were you in the cabin?"

"We had left Buhl to live at Heart Lake. We believed that it was close to the time when there would be big trouble on the earth, and Christians would be persecuted. We also believed that when that happens, we are to flee to the remote areas and even to the mountains." Casey knew that was not the real reason, but it sounded plausible, so he continued. "By we, I mean my wife and me. She was pregnant, so when it was time for the baby to be born, we decided to find a more secure and comfortable place during the winter. That is why we were in the cabin."

"So you admit that it was you that was in the cabin during the last winter?"

"Yes!"

Sheriff David stood and started for the door. "I'll be right back. I need to make a phone call."

Casey remained motionless with no hint of surprise or other emotion. Sheriff Scott and Harry looked at each other with a puzzled look and shrugged their shoulders.

After a few minutes, Sheriff David returned and motioned for Sheriff Scott and Harry to join him in the hall. "I checked with the owner of the cabin and explained the circumstances of the trespass. They decided not to press charges, so I have no reason to hold Mr. Denney here. Also, I don't think we need to bother the Forest Service about the campsite and burn permit. What do you want to do?"

Sheriff Scott thought for a moment and looked at Harry. "We still have the issue with a possible violation of the new birth permit statute, so we will take him back to Twin Falls for further questioning. Besides, I am sure he would feel more comfortable in his own home in Buhl. We also have the problem with the missing wife. Was there foul play, or did she just leave? We still have a missing person or maybe even a homicide. Either way, there are a lot of questions to be answered."

The three returned to the conference room, and Sheriff David gave Casey the good news. "Mr. Denney, the owners of the cabin that you trespassed on have decided not to press charges, so as far as Camas County is concerned, you are free to go. But Sheriff Scott has some additional concerns and is taking you back to Twin Falls County for further questioning. Do you agree to that?"

Casey nodded in agreement. What other choice did he have? He had no place to go, and no way to get there. He couldn't go back to Heart Lake. He would take his chances back in Twin Falls County. The decision left him with a sense of peace because he felt God assuring him that no matter what happened, all would work out according to God's plan. "I agree!"

Ilene met them at the door, kissed John on the forehead, and passed him to Casey. "He was a good baby, didn't fuss at all, and actually slept most of the time. Here are the bottles and the diapers. Good luck!"

As they headed for the SUV, Sheriff Scott hesitated and looked at Harry and Casey. "I know it's late, but I would rather drive to Twin Falls tonight. If you are hungry, we can stop along the way and pick up something."

Harry nodded in agreement. Casey remained silent; it wasn't his decision.

After a little over an hour, they arrived in front of Casey's house in Buhl. The Jeep was in the carport where Casey had instructed Billy to leave it. Casey bundled up John and headed for the front door. Sheriff Scott followed and handed Casey a key. "You will need this to get in. With your parents' permission, we changed the lock. One of my deputies will be here at nine in the morning to bring you to Twin Falls for additional questioning. You can stay here for the night if I have your word that you will cooperate and not try to flee?"

"You have my word."

Casey moved into the house as Sheriff Scott returned to the SUV and drove away. The house was dark, and the lights did not work. He checked the phone, but it was dead. He and Taylor had destroyed their smartphones, so there was no way to communicate with anyone even though he knew he needed to talk to his parents as soon as possible He guessed that his parents had stopped the phone service and shut off the electricity, so he searched and found a battery-powered lantern that they had left behind. He wandered through the house. Not much had been disturbed, and a wave of nostalgia swept through his body. "Taylor, I miss you."

But he couldn't dwell on the past. He had the present and the future to worry about. John needed to be fed and changed, and he was so tired and needed rest. It had been a long, stressful day, and he welcomed the prospect of a deep sleep in his own bed. Tomorrow and its challenges would come all too soon.

John was fed, changed, and lying peacefully on the bed beside him. He had barely dozed off when he heard a voice. "***Casey, be of good faith. You will face some future hardships, but I am with you, and we will overcome those hardships. Be strong in your faith! John will be taken care of. I am your God!***"

As Casey fell into a deep sleep, he felt a new peace. "*I hear You, Lord*!"

On the drive to Twin Falls, Sheriff Scott and Harry agreed that Harry would pick up Casey in the morning. Both would be involved in questioning Casey. As they neared Twin Falls, Harry was impressed to make an unusual offer. "Sheriff, I just had a thought. I don't know why, but I am impressed to consider the baby. And the thought came to me that Amy and I should take care of the baby if Casey is charged and has to be held in prison. Maybe even permanently, if he has to go to prison."

> *"Casey, be of good faith. You will face some future hardships, but I am with you, and we will overcome those hardships. Be strong in your faith! John will be taken care of. I am your God!"*

"Are you sure?"

"I would, of course, need to talk to Amy, but it seemed like there was a voice in my head telling me that was what we should do."

As they drove into the parking lot, Sheriff Scott looked at Harry and muttered, "Weird."

Chapter 28
I Need a Lawyer

"In God I have put my trust: I will not be afraid what man can do to me". (Ps. 56:11, KJV).

At exactly 9:00 a.m., Harry knocked on Casey's door, and Casey opened it. He and John were ready to face the day. They had managed to have a decent breakfast, both had a good night's sleep, and Casey was confident that God was with him. He had decided, however, that he should not be presumptuous. He should rely on God's strength but also use whatever other resources that might be available. He felt the statute requiring a birth permit was unfair and wrong, and he would fight it as much as he could. But he would need a good lawyer.

Therefore, the conversation between Casey and Harry on the drive from Buhl to the sheriff's office in Twin Falls was limited to answers to questions about how the night had been and comments on the scenes along the route to Twin Falls. Upon arrival at the sheriff's office, Harry escorted Casey and John into the conference room. Sam followed and asked Casey if he would like some coffee, water, or something else to drink. Casey declined. Harry and Sam left, leaving Casey sitting at the conference table.

A few minutes later, the sheriff and Harry returned, followed by a woman.

Harry spoke first. "Casey, this is my wife, Amy. If it is alright with you, she will take care of the baby while we have our meeting. She has experience with children. We have a daughter, and so you know I trust her completely. She'll take good care of him."

Remembering the experience with Ilene at the Camas County Sheriff's Office, Casey was quick to respond and offered John to Amy. "That will be fine. His name is John. Here is the bag I packed for him. It has bottles of milk, a change of clothes, and some diapers."

Amy took John in her arms, held him close, and left the room.

Sheriff Scott motioned for Casey and Harry to take a seat around the conference table and once again repeated the Miranda rights. "You have the right to remain silent. Anything you say can and will be used against you in a court of law. You have the right to an attorney. If you cannot afford an attorney, one will be provided for you."

Casey looked first at Sheriff Scott and then at Harry. "I really appreciate your kindness in letting me stay at my home last night and arranging for Amy to take care of John, but after much thought, I have decided to seek the services of an attorney and remain silent until I can have him here with me. I hope you understand. I will also need to make a phone call to see if I can arrange for an attorney."

Sheriff Scott and Harry exchanged glances, and Sheriff Scott firmly responded, "I am not surprised. If I were in your situation, I would have done the same thing. However, that means we will have to place you under arrest, and you may have to stay locked up here until you can arrange for an attorney. Now, just so you understand, John cannot stay with you if you are locked up, but Amy and Harry have offered to take care of John while you are here. Otherwise, John would have to go to Child Protective Services. Do you agree that Amy and Harry can take care of John?"

"Yes, I agree!"

"Are you sure you don't want a court to assign you an attorney in the interim? Maybe we could get this over with, and you could go free."

"No, thank you! I prefer to try to get my own attorney, so I will just have to hope it doesn't take too long.

"Well, then, we will leave and let you make your one phone call."

Sheriff Scott and Harry left the room. "Harry, come join me in my office. I'm going to call the FBI and see what they want us to do." As they went by, he stopped at Sam's desk. "Sam, please get me the FBI office in Boise. Harry and I will be in my office, so I will take it in there."

They moved into Sheriff Scott's office. Sheriff Scott took his seat behind his desk. Harry sat in one of the guest chairs. In a few minutes, Sam poked her head in the office and said, "Line two."

After a lengthy conversation, Sheriff Scott placed the phone on the desk and addressed Harry. "They want us to take care of everything until there is a trial. We can have one of our local judges handle any preliminaries and set bail if it gets that far. We can arrange for a court date as soon as Casey gets his lawyer. In the meantime, if you are in agreement, we let him and the baby stay in his home in Buhl."

"That sounds good to me!"

While Sheriff Scott and Harry were talking to the FBI, Casey had called his parents. His father and mother were full of questions, but Casey insisted that they not talk about anything over the phone. He didn't even tell them about Taylor or John. His father agreed to find a good lawyer and that they would come to Buhl as soon as they could. They wanted to hear what happened.

Sheriff Scott returned to the conference room and presented their decision. "Casey, we talked to the FBI. They have agreed that we can take care of any preliminaries here in Twin Falls. We are going to let you and the baby stay in your home until you can get a lawyer. At that time, we will arrange for a preliminary hearing before a judge here in Twin Falls. What happens after that depends on you and the judge. We expect you to remain in Buhl and check in with us every day, either by phone or in person. Do we have your word that you will do that?"

Casey nodded in agreement.

"Harry will return you and the baby to your home in Buhl. Call us when your lawyer arrives."

Chapter 29

Reunion

> *"Honor your father and your mother, so that you may live long in the land the* Lord *your God is giving you" (Exod. 20:12, NIV).*

Early the next afternoon, there was a knock on Casey's door. When he opened it, he was surprised to see his parents. "Mom, Dad!"

Casey's dad was the first to speak. "Don't look so surprised. Can we come in?"

"Yes. Sure. Yes, come in. I didn't expect you so soon."

Casey's mom gave him a big hug and a kiss on the cheek. "We just couldn't wait. We have been so worried. Why haven't you been in touch? Where is Taylor? I want to give her a big hug too."

There was a cry from the bedroom. Casey's mother gave him a quizzical look and turned toward the bedroom. "What was that?"

"That was John. I'll go get him."

Casey returned with John. "Mom, Dad, this is John, your grandson!"

Both parents had a look of disbelief. Finally, Casey's mother held out her arms, took John in her arms, and looked at Casey. "I don't understand, and where's Taylor?"

> *"Mom, Dad, this is John, your grandson!"*

"It's a long story. Have a seat. Care for anything to drink."

Both declined as they took a seat on the living room couch.

Casey slowly paced the floor as he relayed the story, beginning with learning that Taylor was pregnant and the fact that they did not have a permit and each step of how God had led them into the wilderness at Heart Lake and looked over them as they met each challenge. Casey's mother held John a little tighter and sobbed quietly as he told of the birth of John and the tragic death of Taylor. He spared them the details of her burial except to tell them she was in a safe place, and that he was sure her guardian angel was vigilantly watching over her. He filled them in on what had happened since he was taken into custody by the Twin Falls sheriff and suggested that he might need a lawyer, particularly because of the mysterious absence of Taylor.

Casey's dad agreed and dialed a number on his cell phone. "I need a reference for a good trial lawyer in Twin Falls, Idaho! Dan Gage? Do you have a contact number? Fine, text it to me. Thank you!"

He hung up, checked his messages, and dialed again. "Hello, this is Steven Denney. I would like to speak to Dan Gage. Okay, I'll wait."

"Dan Gage, this is Steven Denney. I would like to meet with you to see if you could represent my son, Casey Denney, in a potential criminal case. If we could meet, we can explain more in detail. Fine, we can meet you at your office this evening. Seven okay? The address? Good. See you there."

"I'm famished. Let's go get something to eat. Marie can stay here with John, and Casey, you and I can meet with the lawyer. Are you supposed to keep the sheriff informed?"

Marie spoke up. "Casey, before we do anything else, you need to call your brother and sister and Taylor's parents. I'm sure that Brady and Kayla have been very worried about you and would like to hear what happened. And Taylor's parents deserve to hear the story from you also."

"Dad, can I use your phone?" Casey dialed. "Hey, bro. What's happening? Yes, I'm okay. It's a long story. Let's just say I may be in trouble with the law and could use your prayers. I'll tell you the whole story when I see you. Everything okay at Southern? Good to hear your voice. Talk to you later."

Casey dialed again. "How's my favorite sister? Yes, I'm fine! Don't worry, Mom and Dad are here, and I have a good lawyer. No, there's nothing you need to do except pray for me. By the way, you have a little nephew. Taylor? She died at the birth. I know, it was so sad, and I miss her so, but she is safe, sleeping until the resurrection. Stay strong. We all want to be there together some day. Love you too!"

Casey hesitated. "Mom, I know I need to call Taylor's parents, but I have been dreading it ever since she died. But here goes!" He paused a moment and then dialed. "This is Casey." When he hung up, the color had drained from his face. "They didn't take it well, and I know they must hate me. I let their only daughter die! I don't know if they will ever forgive me. All I can do is trust in God and let Him work it out. I know that when Jesus comes that Taylor and I will be reunited, and I hope that her parents will also be there to join in that reunion for eternity." He put his face in his hands, sobbing as tears ran down his cheeks.

Casey regained his composure. "I should give Sheriff Scott a call."

After talking to the sheriff, they headed for the best restaurant in Buhl, "Old Home Cooking."

Chapter 30

The Arraignment

*"Acquitting the guilty and condemning the innocent—
the* Lord *detests them both" (Prov. 17:15, NIV).*

Casey and his father arrived at the lawyer's office as scheduled and were ushered into a large conference room by the office receptionist. A few minutes later, Dan Gage and a young lady entered the room.

"Good evening. I'm Dan Gage, and this is Debra Green, my para-legal." As he shook Casey's hand, he continued, "You must be Casey?" He then addressed Casey's father. "And you must be Steven Denney. The first thing we need to do is address our fee schedule. Here is a summary sheet. Take your time and look it over. If you wish, we can step out and give you some time to go over it."

Steve quickly responded. "That won't be necessary. From what I see, your fees are satisfactory, and we can agree. Where do I sign?"

"Good, then we can get started, but I will have to ask you, Steven, to step out so that Casey can give us the entire story. I don't know how much he has told you, but we don't want you to have any additional information because you do not have lawyer-client privilege and could be called by the prosecution to testify.

"I understand. I'll be out in the reception area."

"Now, Casey, tell me what happened. Start from the beginning, and give me as much detail as you can. Try not to leave anything out. Nothing is insignificant or unimportant."

Casey talked for over an hour, relating in detail the events that began with the realization that Taylor was pregnant and ending with the apprehension at Heart Lake and the interrogation at the Camas County Sheriff's Office. "I think that's the whole story."

"Are you sure you haven't left anything out?"

"I'm sure!"

"So, you admitted during the interrogation that you had stayed at the cabin during the winter, but you didn't confess to anything else, not even that your wife had died? But it was obvious that you were in possession of a baby. And you did not have a child-bearing permit?"

"That's right."

"Have you told anyone else about what happened?"

"I told my parents and Taylor's parents."

"The whole story, including how Taylor had died."

"Yes!"

"Have you told anyone where she is buried?"

"No, and I doubt anyone can find her because when the sheriffs found me, they had dogs with them, and the dogs gave no sign that they could detect that she was there. I believe God will protect her and not let anyone find her."

"Well, you probably can expect to be charged for violating the international statute/treaty that prohibits fathering a child without a valid birth permit. I'm not sure what they will do about the missing wife-mother. We will just have to wait and see if they want to press charges on that issue. We have an arraignment hearing set for 9:00 a.m. day after tomorrow. I will review what we discussed today and see you at 8:30 for the hearing in Twin Falls at the District Court, 427 Shoshone Street."

"We'll be there. Thank you so much for taking my case on such short notice."

"You're welcome. I am glad to do it. I'll see you tomorrow."

Casey left the conference room, met his father in the reception area, and exited the building.

"Son, how did it go? Are you okay with him as your lawyer?"

"Sure, Dad. And we are to meet him at 8:30 a.m. day after tomorrow at the District Court in Twin Falls for an arraignment hearing."

"Casey, I am going to call the General Conference tomorrow. This is a religious freedom issue, and they should be involved."

With that, neither one spoke on the drive to Buhl.

Casey and his father arrived at the District Court precisely at 8:30. Dan Gage was there to greet them in the hallway outside the courtroom. Steve Denney pulled Dan aside. "There is something I need to let you know. Casey is a member of the Seventh-day Adventist Church, as are most of his family. The Seventh-day Adventist Church is a big advocate for religious freedom, and we have a large department of legal experts in Maryland that work with and defend those of our members whose religious rights are being violated. I believe that this case is clearly an issue of exercising religious freedom. Yesterday, I contacted the General Conference, and they agreed with my conclusion. So, if this goes to trial, they have agreed to give you whatever assistance you may need. It's your choice, however, and it will be up to you whether or not to use their resources. They would even send a religious freedom lawyer to assist you if you wanted. I thought you should know this upfront, and if it is a problem, we need to address it before we go in today."

Dan quickly responded. "No problem, I am happy to use whatever and whoever we need to win the case and make Casey a free man. Let's go in the courtroom."

Casey and Dan took seats at the defense table, and Steve sat down in the row behind them. Dan and the prosecutor exchanged glances, but neither spoke. Right at 9:00, the bailiff stood up and declared, "All rise. The Federal District Court of the State of Idaho is now in session, the Honorable Judge, Derrick K. Walkman presiding."

The Arraignment 113

Judge Walkman entered the courtroom and took his seat behind the bench.

The bailiff recited the docket number, declared that the case was, "The State of Idaho versus Casey Denney," and instructed all to be seated.

Judge Walkman appeared to finish reading something on his desk, looked up, and spoke. "Will the defendant please rise and state your name."

Casey rose. "Casey Denney."

"Is the gentleman beside you the lawyer you have selected to defend you?"

"Yes, Your Honor."

"And has he instructed you of your rights and the procedure that we will follow in this courtroom?"

"Yes, Your Honor."

"You are charged with two crimes. The first is violation of the International Birth Control Act, to wit, fathering a baby without the proper birth permit from the Department of Homeland Security. How do you plead?"

Dan Gage spoke up. "Your Honor, we plead not guilty!"

"The second crime you are charged with is Criminal Negligent Homicide in the death of one Taylor Denney. How do you plead?"

Casey was visibly shaken as Dan Gage responded. "Your Honor, we plead not guilty!"

"Very well, Casey Denney, you are remanded to the Twin Falls County Sheriff for incarceration until trial."

"Your Honor, I request that my client be allowed to be free under his own cognizance until trial."

The prosecution immediately objected. "Your Honor, the defendant should at least post bail. He has already demonstrated a willingness to disappear into the wilderness to avoid the law."

"Very well, bail is set for $50,000, and the defendant is under the custody of the Twin Falls County Sheriff until such time as bail is posted. Also, the defendant is not allowed to leave Twin Falls County until the trial is completed. Court is adjourned."

Casey was ushered out by the sheriff's deputy. Steve Denney left to get the bail. By mid-afternoon, Casey was free, and they headed back to Buhl with a promise from Dan Gage to be in touch in a few days.

Chapter 31
Trial – The Prosecution

"For I am convinced that neither death nor life, neither angels or demons, neither the present or the future, nor any powers, neither height nor depth, nor anything else in all creation, will be able to separate us from the love of God that is in Christ Jesus our Lord" (Rom. 8:38–39, NIV).

"All rise. The Federal District Court of the State of Idaho is now in session, the Honorable Judge, Derrick K. Walkman presiding."

Judge Walkman entered the courtroom and took his seat behind the bench.

The bailiff continued. "You may be seated." He recited the case number. "The United States of America versus Casey Denney!"

Judge Walkman instructed the bailiff. "Please bring in the jury pool." When the final member of the jury pool had taken a seat, Judge Walkman turned to face the prosecutor. "You may begin the jury selection."

After the final member of the jury had been selected, which had taken most of the day, the judge declared that court was adjourned and that they would reconvene the next day at 9:00 a.m.

The jury was fairly well-balanced between the few selected by the prosecutor who expressed a willingness to be sympathetic to those who believed that people were the major contributor to global climate change and that a higher Being had no place in the cause or solution, and the few selected by the defense that believed that there was a God, He was in control of the universe, and people had very little, if any, part or power in the regulation of earth's climate. The rest of the jury declared that they had no opinion either way.

After resuming session the next day, Judge Walkman addressed the prosecution. "Do you wish to make an opening statement?"

"Yes, Your Honor."

"Proceed."

"Ladies and gentlemen of the jury, thank you for your willingness to serve on this landmark case. A case that has the attention of the entire nation because it has far-reaching consequences for the salvation of our lifestyle as we know it, and perhaps, our very existence on this earth. According to a majority of experts, we face a drastic change in our ecosystem due to climate change, and our national leaders have passed a law to stem the on-rushing calamities due to climate change by limiting population growth. We will prove that Casey Denney is guilty of breaking that law by fathering a child without the proper permit, as called for by the law. We will also prove beyond a shadow of doubt that Casey Denney is guilty of negligent homicide in the death of the mother of the child, one Taylor Denney. We will prove that Casey Denney was aware of the risks associated with the actions that led to Taylor Denney's death, that Casey Denney failed to act appropriately in a dangerous situation that caused the death of Taylor Denney, and that there is a direct link between Casey Denney's conduct and the death of Taylor Denney."

> *We will prove that Casey Denney is guilty of breaking that law by fathering a child without the proper permit, as called for by the law.*

"Does the defense wish to respond?"

"Yes, thank you, Your Honor. Ladies and gentlemen of the jury. Casey Denney is a law-abiding citizen of the State of Idaho. He had never been arrested. He has never been convicted of any crime. He has not even had a parking ticket. He was a good student, got an education, and worked hard. He married his high school sweetheart. Paid his taxes. He was living the American dream. He believes in God, is a member in good standing of the Twin Falls Seventh-day Adventist Church, and serves his God in many ways. He also believes he has a duty to obey God's commands even when they conflict with man's laws. His God said *be fruitful and replenish the earth,* and Casey believes that his religious liberty as protected under the U. S. Constitution was violated by the population control law.

Judge Walkman instructed the prosecution to call its first witness.

"Thank you, Judge, the prosecution calls Twin Falls County Sheriff, Darrin Scott."

Sheriff Scott took the stand and was sworn in.

"Do you swear to tell the truth and nothing but the truth?"

"I do!"

The prosecution began. "Sheriff Scott, will you please tell the court the circumstances that led to the arrest of the defendant, Casey Denney?"

Sheriff Scott recited the entire story, beginning with the call from Betty Johnson at the Main Street Book Store, followed by the attempt to identify and locate Casey Denney, the tip from the Camas County Sheriff, and the subsequent apprehension of Casey Denney at Heart Lake.

"What did you find at Heart Lake?"

"We found a primitive campsite, and Casey Denney holding a baby. There was also a nanny goat." The judge and jury smiled at the mention of the nanny goat, but the prosecution did not dig deeper into the issue of the nanny goat.

"Who is we?"

"Myself, my deputy Harry Mason, the Camas County Sheriff Sandy David, and his deputy. We also had some tracking dogs with us."

"Did Casey Denney try to hide, flee, or resist arrest?"

"Oh, no! He was very cooperative and willingly allowed us to take him to the Camas County Sheriff's Office for questioning."

"Did Casey Denney say anything about who the baby belonged to or whether there was a mother involved?"

"Not at that time. But later, when we questioned him at the Camas County Sheriff's Office, he informed us that there had been three of them living at the cabin, the baby, his wife. and himself."

"Did he have a certified birth permit for the baby in his possession?"

"Not that I am aware of, but we didn't ask him for one at that time."

"Well, Sheriff Scott, did you ever determine whether the defendant had a valid, certified birth permit issued by Homeland Security?"

"He never produced one, and in later questioning in Twin Falls, he admitted that he did not have one."

"Is it possible to assume, then, that the reason Casey Denney and his wife were at Heart Lake was a premeditated attempt to avoid the punishment called for in the statute forbidding having a baby without a valid certified birth permit?"

"Objection, Your Honor, calls for speculation!"

"Objection sustained, clerk, please strike the question from the record."

"No further questions, Your Honor!"

"Attorney for the defense, do you wish to question the witness?"

"Sheriff Scott, first let me thank you for your service as a law enforcement officer. Did you observe any evidence that indicated that there had been any foul play or criminal negligent homicide at the campsite at Heart Lake?"

"We found no such evidence."

"Did the tracking dogs indicate whether there were human remains at the campsite at Heart Lake?"

"Not that I am aware of, but I am not an expert at recognizing signals from tracking dogs. You will have to ask Sandy Davis about that. They were his dogs."

"No further questions, Your Honor."

"Does the prosecution wish to redirect?"

"No, Your Honor."

"Sheriff Scott, you may step down. The prosecution may call its next witness."

"The prosecution calls Betty Johnson to the stand."

"Ms. Johnson, you are under oath. Are you the owner of the Main Street Book Store in Twin Falls, Idaho?"

"Yes, I am and have been for several years. It has gotten tougher and tougher to make a living selling books, what with all the books available on the internet. And it seems people have less and less interest in reading books; too much other stuff is available online and on TV."

"I understand, but do you remember selling two books to a certain young man, oh, say within the last two years?"

"I certainly do!"

"Now, Ms. Johnson, look carefully, is that young man present in this courtroom?"

"He certainly is, and he's sitting right over there by the man with the red, white, and blue tie!"

"Let the record indicate that Ms. Johnson referred to Casey Denney as the one sitting by the man in the red, white, and blue tie, the defendant's lawyer. And Ms. Johnson, what were the two books that Casey Denney purchased at your book store?"

"One was on wilderness living, and the other was a guide for midwifery."

"Ms. Johnson, why would a young man like Casey Denney purchase a guide for midwifery?"

"He must have been planning to deliver a baby sometime!"

Dan Gage immediately rose from his chair. "Objection, calls for speculation. Ms. Johnson is neither an expert on delivering a baby or mind reader."

"Objection sustained. Any further questions?"

"The prosecution has no further questions."

"Counsel for the defense do you wish to question the witness?"

"No, Your Honor."

The prosecution calls Sheriff Sandy David to the stand."

After Sandy David was sworn in, the prosecution continued. "Sheriff David, please describe to the jury why last spring you were called to investigate a particular summer cabin along the South Fork of the Boise River?"

"I would be happy to. The owners called our office to complain of a possible break-in of the cabin and reported that their dog had dug up a bag in the backyard that had some suspicious contents."

"Did you investigate?"

"Yes, sir, the very next day."

"And what did you find?"

"We visited the cabin and retrieved the suspicious bag. The bag contained bedsheets and towels that were bloodstained, and other items that a doctor in Fairfield confirmed were items consistent with the birth of a child."

"Your Honor, we have a sworn statement from the doctor in Fairfield that we would like to place into evidence and an inventory of the contents of the bag found at the cabin."

"Defense, do you have any objection?"

"No, Your Honor."

The prosecution continued. "Sheriff David, what happened next in your investigation?"

"I called Sheriff Scott. I had a hunch. He had distributed an all-points bulletin to be on the lookout for a missing person suspected to be Casey Denney. I thought maybe Casey had used the cabin to hide over the winter, and Sheriff Scott suggested he join us in a search of the area. Four of us, Sheriff Scott and his deputy along with one of my deputies, searched the area from the cabin for several miles up the river. We used all-terrain vehicles and dogs."

"Did you find Casey Denney?"

"Yes, he was up a canyon that started where the road ended. He was at a campsite along the stream from Heart Lake that had a shelter, rustic furniture, and a firepit. He just stood there with a baby in his arms as we approached. We asked if he would come with us to our office for questioning. He agreed, and we went directly to our office. He did not offer any resistance and was very cooperative."

"Were there any vehicles at or around the campsite or at the cabin that had been broken in to?"

"We did not find any."

"What did you learn during the questioning?"

"He admitted that he was the one that had used the cabin during the winter. But, when we asked about his wife, he just said she was gone, or left, or something like that. I called the owners of the cabin, and they decided not to press charges, so Sheriff Scott took jurisdiction, and they all left."

"Did you ask him about the bag the dog found at the cabin?"

"No, we decided to keep that under wraps until we could get an analysis done on the blood and other items. We submitted the contents of the bag to a forensic lab in Boise for a complete analysis, including DNA. During the questioning at our office, my secretary took care of the baby, and per my instructions got a sample of the baby's hair and a swab of saliva from the nipple of the bottle she used to feed him. Sheriff Scott also managed to get a sample from Casey Denney for analysis."

"What were the results of the lab analysis?"

"The DNA test showed that Casey Denney was the father of the baby. The other tests showed that the blood and other specimens on the sheets and towels were consistent with the birth of a baby. Also, the DNA tests indicated that the blood was that of Taylor Denney, the defendant's wife."

"Where did you get a specimen of Taylor's DNA to compare with the DNA in the blood?

"Taylor's parents gave us a lock of Taylor's hair that they had kept from her first haircut."

"Were you able to determine anything else from the blood on the sheets and towels?"

"Not really, we would have liked to get an idea of the quantity of blood, but that wasn't possible."

"No further questions, Your Honor."

"Does the defense wish to cross-examine?"

"Yes, Your Honor. Sheriff David, did you find any evidence that would conclusively show that there had been any foul play or negligent criminal homicide at either the cabin or the campsite at Heart Lake? Did you find any human body or remains that were identified as that of Taylor Denney?"

"We did not. We went back to the cabin and the campsite with our dogs to see if we could locate any human remains, and the dogs detected nothing. Funny thing happened, though, the last time we were at the campsite. A man was there. Big guy! Had a white beard and strange-looking eyes, sort of penetrating, like he could see right through you. He wasn't bothering anything, so we didn't make an issue of it, but it looked like he might be sticking around for a while. Strange, too; the dogs seemed to take a liking to him."

"No further questions, Your Honor."

"The witness may step down. Any more witnesses for the prosecution?"

"Yes, Your Honor, the prosecution calls Dr. Lori Standmier."

Dr. Standmier took the witness stand and was sworn in.

"Dr. Standmier, please tell the jury what your specialty is and why you are here."

"Sure! I am a medical OB/GYN doctor with a practice in Boise, Idaho. I am also a consultant for the lab that analyzed the contents of the bag found at the cabin along the South Fork of the Boise River. Of course, I have treated many pregnant women and delivered dozens of babies."

"Doctor, based on your professional opinion and your examination of the contents of the subject bag, what took place at the cabin occupied by the defendant?"

"In my expert opinion, a baby was born at or near the cabin. Probably in the cabin because of the presence of the blood-stained sheets and towels that the owners insisted were those in the cabin."

"Doctor, in your expert opinion, how would you assess the risk for life-threatening consequences for a human birth in the cabin environment?"

"I would rate the risk and likelihood of life-threatening consequences as very high, particularly because of the absence of professional medical assistance if there were complications and the distance from any such assistance. Because of the amount of blood on the sheets and towels, I conclude that there were life-threatening consequences at the birth."

"Doctor, one more question. Is there anything in the testimonies you have heard so far that would indicate that the father of the child was willing to assume the risk of any life-threatening consequences in the birth at the cabin?"

"Yes! To me, the fact that the defendant purchased a book on midwifery indicates a willingness to have an unassisted birth and assume whatever risk there might be."

"No further questions, Your Honor."

"Counsel for the defense, do you wish to cross-examine the witness?"

"Yes, Your Honor. Doctor, what evidence do you have that the mother of the child born at the cabin is deceased?"

"I merely testified that, based on the amount of blood on the sheets and towels, that there is a high probability that she is."

"But, you have no positive proof beyond the shadow of a doubt?"

"That's correct!"

"And you have no evidence that the mother did not also accept equal risk for the circumstances of the birth of the child in the remote cabin?"

"Correct, I have no proof that she did or did not."

"Thank you, doctor, no further questions."

"Does the prosecution wish to call additional witnesses?"

"No, Your Honor, the prosecution rests."

"Okay, since the hour is late, court is adjourned until 9:00 tomorrow morning.

Attorney Gage caught Casey's parents before they left the courtroom and suggested the four of them meet in the coffee shop across the street from the courthouse. After ordering some refreshments and taking a seat, attorney Gage opened the conversation. "I feel that things are going well and that the prosecution has not presented a strong case, but we have to decide whether Casey should testify. There are some facts of this case that only Casey knows about, and so far, the prosecution has not been able to prove them, so my recommendation would be that he not. But I will be happy to hear your input."

Casey's father was the first to speak. "We trust your judgment, so my vote would be to not have Casey testify."

"How about you, Casey?"

"I, too, trust your judgment and agree."

"Marie?"

"I agree!"

"Good, then we will rely on outside witnesses for our defense and pray that God will give the jury the wisdom to see and understand why Casey is innocent. Steven, would you offer a prayer?"

> *"Good, then we will rely on outside witnesses for our defense and pray that God will give the jury the wisdom to see and understand why Casey is innocent."*

Chapter 32
Trial – The Defense

> *"Awake, and rise to my defense! Contend for
> me, my God and Lord" (Ps. 35:23, NIV).*

"Counsel for the defense, you may call your first witness."

"The defense calls Sergeant Jay Hamilton."

Sergeant Hamilton took the witness stand and was sworn in.

"Sergeant Hamilton, please tell the jury your position and your relationship to the defendant."

"I am a member of the Buhl, Idaho, police department. I have known the defendant ever since he was in high school. I was a big booster of the Buhl High School athletics and enjoyed watching the school's teams, and in particular, Casey's play. He was very good and always a good sport that followed the rules of the games."

"As a member of the Buhl police force, did you ever give Casey a ticket or have to arrest him?"

"No, never; he was always a law-abiding citizen while in school as well as when he came back to Buhl after college."

"What about Casey's wife? Was she also a law-abiding citizen?

"I certainly haven't known her as long as Casey, but I do know she was never in trouble with our department and appeared to be as law-abiding as Casey."

"No further questions."

"Does the prosecution wish to cross-examine?"

"Yes, Your Honor. Sergeant Hamilton. Is it true that Casey Denney was an avid participant in risky activities, such as snowboarding, on the most challenging ski resorts in North America?"

"Yes!"

"And extreme wakeboarding."

"Yes!"

"And surfing in the ocean?"

"And skydiving?"

"Yes!"

"And how are you aware of Casey's risky activities?"

"During the summer before his freshman year of college, Casey came to our office to get our signature on a background form for attending a semester in a college in Australia. I asked him why he was going to Australia. His reason was that he wanted to surf in the ocean off the coast of Australia. We talked about the risk of surfing, and he told me he felt it was no more risky than some of the other things he had done, snowboarding, wakeboarding, and skydiving."

"From that conversation, you concluded that Casey was bent on trying almost anything, regardless of the risk and the consequences?"

"Objection, the prosecution is leading the witness!"

"Overruled."

"Thank you, Your Honor. Sergeant Hamilton?"

"Yes, that was my conclusion."

"No further questions."

"Counsel for the defense, do you have any further questions for the witness."

"Yes, Your Honor. Sergeant Hamilton, was the time you and Casey had that conversation ever repeated?"

"No."

"Are you aware whether Casey has continued and is presently participating in those specific risky activities you described, or any other risky activities?"

"Not that I am aware of."

"Thank you, no further questions."

"Prosecution?"

"No further questions."

"Defense, you may call your next witness."

"The defense calls Pastor Kaufman."

Pastor Kaufman took the stand and was sworn in.

"Pastor Kaufman, what church do you pastor, and how long have you been a pastor there?"

"Twin Falls Seventh-day Adventist Church. I have been a pastor there for ten years."

"Is the defendant, Casey Denney, a member of your church?

"Yes, he is a member."

"How long has he been a member?"

"He has been a member since he was baptized, which I believe was when he was twelve, although I was not the pastor when he was baptized."

"How would you describe Casey Denney as a member of your church?"

"I would describe him as faithful to the church and to Jesus."

"What do you mean by that?"

"From my observation as his pastor, he believes that Jesus is his Savior and that he should try to follow God's laws as best he could through the grace of Jesus."

"What do you mean by the term God's laws?"

"Well, God's commandments, including the Ten Commandments and the ones Jesus gave us while He was here on this earth. Actually, Jesus and God are of one mind, and so God's commandments are considered to also be in harmony with Jesus's commandments. The Bible says that -'In the beginning was the Word, and the Word was with God, and the Word was God. He was with God in the beginning' (John 1:1–2, NIV). So Jesus was there at Creation and at the making of man and woman (see Gen. 1:26)."

"What was the first commandment that God slash Jesus gave to man?"

"You will find that in Genesis 1:28, 'God blessed them and said to them, "Be fruitful and increase in number; fill the earth and subdue it." So God was saying to the man and woman have offspring, have babies."

"Would you say, then, that the law that Casey is accused of breaking, the forbidding of having children without permission from the State, is in direct conflict with God's commandments, and that Casey and his wife were merely doing what they thought God wanted them to do? They were exercising their basic right to religious freedom granted by the constitution of the United States?"

"Yes, I believe that to be true."

"No further questions, Your Honor."

"Prosecution, do you wish to question the witness?"

"Yes, Your Honor. Pastor Kaufman, can you say that Casey Denney and his wife always obeyed God's commandments and never broke even one?"

"No, I can't say that, because we have all sinned, which is defined by the Bible as the transgression or breaking of God's laws. I have sinned, and probably, Counselor, you have too. But that doesn't mean we should not do our best through the grace of Jesus to obey God's laws rather than man's if they conflict."

"Pastor, can you honestly say that when Casey Denney was in the act of getting his wife pregnant, the only thought in his mind was, I am doing what God wants me to do?"

The spectators in the court who had been sitting quietly, burst out in laughter.

"Order in the court."

"Pastor, what is your answer."

"I have no way of knowing what he was thinking, but that was probably low on the priority list."

"No further questions."

"The defense calls Ted Garland."

Ted Garland took the stand and was sworn in.

"Mr. Garland, please tell the jury your profession and your area of expertise."

"I am a lawyer. I currently am associate general counsel for the General Conference of the Seventh-day Adventist Church. I specialize in religious freedom issues as guaranteed under the Constitution of the United States."

"Do you consider this case a religious freedom issue?"

"Yes, I do, and I think that Pastor Kaufman's testimony stated the case very well! This issue of restricting and criminalizing the right to have children is just one of the ways our religious liberty is being eroded."

"What other ways are you suggesting?"

"There are several, including the new Sunday law, which prohibits the conducting of any business on Sunday. Our church believes that God sanctified Saturday as the Sabbath, and for our mental and physical well-being, commanded that we rest on the Sabbath. So our members do not work on Saturday. Now, with the Sunday law, they cannot conduct their business on Sunday as well. This places an unfair economic disadvantage on our members. Some politicians have felt the law also requires worship only on Sunday. This would place an unfair spiritual burden on our members. Also, several states have recently passed legislation forbidding pastors or other church members from counseling members or nonmembers who wish to change a lifestyle or overcome behavior they consider a sin. Then, there is the issue of the definition of marriage. So far, our pastors have not been required to perform a marriage for anyone other than a man and a woman, but we fear that may also be changed by legislation."

"Thank you, Mr. Garland. No further questions."

"Prosecution?"

"Mr. Garland, isn't it true that a lot of the members of the Seventh-day Adventist Church do work on Saturday?"

"Yes, they do, but those that do primarily work for medical facilities, such as hospitals that provide medical care to patients round the clock seven days a week."

"Do those medical facilities also have business offices that are not directly related to the care of patients, and do those offices shut down on Saturday?"

"Yes, those medical facilities have business offices, and to my knowledge, do not shut down on Saturday. It is a convenience for the patients."

"So, if I hear you correctly, there are times when your church members do not follow God's laws when it is convenient and for the common good? No further questions!"

"Does the defense counsel wish to redirect?

"Yes, Your Honor. Mr. Garland, who gave us the laws found in the Bible?"

"Jesus."

"And who in the Bible was known to heal the sick, comfort the downtrodden, and do good on the Sabbath?"

"Jesus."

"No further questions. Your Honor, the defense rests."

"We will break for lunch, and counselors, when we reconvene, you may give the jury your closing statements."

Chapter 33
Trial – The Verdict

*"Vindicate me in your righteousness, O LORD my God;
do not let them gloat over me" (Ps. 35:24, NIV).*

"Court is now in session. Counsel for the prosecution, you may make your closing statement."

"Thank you, Your Honor. Ladies and gentlemen of the jury, you have a clear decision to make in this case. Did Casey Denney violate the law requiring a birth permit to father a child? The prosecution has proved that Casey Denney did father a child without the required birth permit. Now, the defense would have you believe that Casey Denney's actions were legal because they were directed by a commandment from God, and the birth permit law is a restriction on his constitutional right to religious freedom and expression. The Supreme Court has ruled that laws like the birth permit law are constitutional and do not limit a single person's religious liberty because they protect and promote the common good. The United States is not a Judeo-Christian nation, even though some of our laws have a Judeo-Christian foundation. But the United States is a secular nation, and our legislation makes laws for the common good no matter the foundation. Mankind needed to act quickly to prevent global climate change from destroying the planet and our way of life. Population control was considered the most effective and manageable way to achieve that goal. It was done for the common good, so we must punish those who disdain the common good. Casey Denney clearly acted selfishly and disdained the common good. Casey Denney must have realized that he and his wife had broken the law because they fled to the mountains to avoid arrest and prosecution. Which brings us to the other charge against Casey Denney, criminal negligent homicide."

"Casey Denney is also guilty of criminal negligent homicide because:

"One, he was known to be a risk-taker and was aware of the risks associated with the actions he took that ultimately led to his wife's death. He took her to a remote location in the mountains away from the safety of their home and community, knowing that there were no medical facilities close enough to have provided the medical care his wife needed in the highly risky birth of a child. He did so by not even providing any means of transportation that would have even a glimmer of hope of getting his wife to medical treatment. In fact, he completely ignored the fact that childbirth under the best conditions is risky, but thought by reading a book on midwifery, he could take matters into his own hands."

"Two, he failed to act appropriately in a dangerous situation, and that act or lack of acting caused his wife's death. Who knows what actually happened in that cabin during the birth, but it is obvious that Casey Denney was not equipped or had the skills to manage the situation in a way that would save his wife's life."

"Three, there is a direct link between the defendant's conduct and his wife's death, as evidenced by his decision to relocate to a remote mountain location to avoid arrest and prosecution."

"You must find Casey Denney guilty on both counts, the evidence is clear, and the law demands it."

"Counsel for the defense?"

"Thank you, Your Honor. Ladies and gentlemen of the jury, you must find the defendant Casey Denney innocent of these charges. Casey Denney has been a law-abiding and model member of his community for his entire life, and with one moment of love for his wife and in harmony with the God of the Universe's admonition to be fruitful and multiply, his wife got pregnant. It was their religious right to do so, and the birth permit law truly denies them that right. The mere fact that the law exists caused them to panic and flee to the mountains to protect the unborn child. Sure, that was a risky decision, but we have no evidence that Casey's wife, Taylor, was not in full agreement to take that risk. As the prosecution has stated, we don't know what happened in that cabin where the baby was born. In fact, the prosecution has presented no evidence that, indeed, Casey's wife Taylor is, in reality, deceased. They have found no body and no evidence of foul play. All we have is a statement by the defendant that she left. You can't blame him for trying to protect her as much as possible. There is no evidence that suggests that Casey is guilty of negligent homicide. Thank you!"

"Ladies and gentlemen of the jury, you have heard the evidence and arguments by the prosecution and the defense. The bailiff will escort you to the jury room to begin your deliberations. Court is now adjourned until the jury has reached a decision."

Casey, his parents, and Dan Gage gathered in an anteroom to await the verdict. All four just sat in silence for over an hour, each with his own thoughts about the trial.

Casey's dad was the first to speak. "Well, Dan, how do you think it went, and how do you read the jury?"

"Frankly, I think it went well. During my closing statement, I could sense some sympathy in some of the jury, and I expect that it will take some time for them to reach a verdict. I didn't see any of the jurors look away or look down at their hands; they all looked right at me. I think they will especially have a hard time with the homicide charge since there is no real proof that there was a homicide. Someday, Casey, you will have to tell me what really happened at the cabin."

Casey did not respond.

"I tend to agree with you, Dan, but if Casey is found guilty, we will appeal the verdict to the highest court. I have to still believe that religious liberty is still alive in the United States."

"No, Dad, if I am convicted, I really don't want to appeal. I will take my punishment, do the time, and move on. I have faith that God will take care of me even in prison, and if that is where I must go to serve Him, I will. If that happens, I wish you would spend your effort on seeing that John is okay and well taken care of. I know the state will take custody of him, but I hope you can maintain contact in some way to let him know that I love him. I have faith that someday we will all be reunited when Jesus returns. The way the world is going that can't be that far off!"

"Son, if that is your wish, we will honor it and try hard to stay in John's life if the government will allow it."

"Thanks, Dad, and Mom, thank you for all your support and being the best mother I could ever want. I love you! Dad, will you say a prayer for Taylor, John, and me?"

They had just finished praying when Dan's cell phone rang. "That was the bailiff. We have to return to the courtroom. The jury has reached a verdict."

Casey and Dan took their seats at the defense table, while Steve and Marie sat behind them in the gallery. Marie reached over the railing and patted Casey on the shoulder.

"All rise. The Federal District Court of Idaho is now in session, the Honorable Derrick K. Walkman presiding."

"You may be seated. Bailiff, please retrieve the jury."

Dan Gage eyed each of the jurors as they filed in and took their seats and whispered to Casey, "Hard to tell!"

"Members of the jury, have you reached a verdict?"

A middle-aged, gray-haired man rose. "We have your honor."

The bailiff took a piece of paper and handed it to the judge. After examining the sheet of paper, the judge asked," Defendant, please rise. What is your verdict?"

"Judge, on the first count of fathering a child without a valid birth permit, we find the defendant guilty."

"On the second count of criminal negligent homicide, we find the defendant guilty."

There was a gasp of shock in the courtroom, and Marie began to cry.

"Bailiff, please take the defendant into custody. Casey Denney, you are remanded to the custody of the Twin Falls County Sheriff to await a sentencing hearing. Court is dismissed!"

A few days later, Casey was back in court for the sentencing. He was sentenced to seventeen years in the Idaho State prison, ten years for fathering a child without a birth permit, and seven years for criminal negligent homicide.

Chapter 34
The Outreach

"Religion that God our Father accepts as pure and faultless is this: to look after orphans and widows in their distress" (James 1:27, NIV).

Brady Denney enjoyed his work in the Physical Education Department at Southern Adventist University. He loved to work with young people. In fact, he spent many years as a counselor at a youth camp in the area while in college, and his new venture also involved young men. Some of his students at the university had urged him to check out the new church in the area. It was called "The Crossgate." They were excited about it and the program it offered them. It met on Sabbath morning, and though the leaders had Seventh-day Adventist roots, it was not a traditional Seventh-day Adventist Church. The worship service also was not traditional, but more like the typical non-denominational church with lively music accompanied by drums, guitars, and an occasional cymbal. The main emphasis for this church, however, was not so much the worship service but the philosophy. They were organized to serve the community, and that is what immediately appealed to Brady. He signed up as a mentor at the Federal Orphanage just outside Chattanooga, Tennessee.

On his first day at the orphanage, he was assigned to a young man named John. They took seats in the chapel, and Brady opened the conversation. "Hi. My name is Brady. If you like, we can spend a few moments together each week, no agenda, just being friends and getting acquainted. How does that sound?"

"Okay, I guess." Not showing a lot of enthusiasm or interest.

"Good, let's start by my telling you a little bit about me, and you can tell me a little bit about you. Sound okay?"

"Yeah."

> *On his first day at the orphanage, he was assigned to a young man named John.*

Brady spent several minutes telling John about his family, his work, and what he liked to do. "Now, John, what can you tell me about you."

"Not much."

"Well, what can you tell me about your life here at the orphanage?"

"It sucks, and just as soon as I can, I'm out of here!"

"That bad?"

"You bet it's bad, and I've had enough of it—the people, the rules, and especially the food."

"How long have you been here?"

"Seventeen years, I think. I think I was brought here as a baby and have been here ever since."

"Do you know anything about your parents, your family."

"Nope, and I really don't care!"

"I guess I don't blame you. Well, I think I will go and let you get back to whatever you usually do. Would you like me to come back?"

"If you want to. I'll be here with nothing better to do!"

"Okay, I'll see you next week."

The next week, Brady decided that he would share his faith with John and see how he would respond. As usual, they met in the chapel and exchanged some chit-chat about the past week and how things were going before Brady made his move. "John, I have a present for you."

There was no response from John, so Brady handed him a small package. "Go ahead, John; open it."

John eyed first Brady and then the package suspiciously before hesitantly opening one end of the wrapping. "What's this?"

"John, it's a Bible. I thought you might like to have one. Have you ever read the Bible? Do you know what it is about?"

John stared first at Brady, then at the Bible, and back at Brady. "No, I've never had one, and all I know is some of the guys in here read it a lot and have tried to get me to read one, but I wasn't interested."

"Would you like to know more about it?"

"I think so if you will help me."

"I'll be more than happy to help you and guide you in a study of the plan that the Bible outlines for all of us. The promise of eternal life in heaven. Interested?"

"Sure, when do we start?"

"Right now!"

Brady and John studied the Bible together for several weeks. John was a good and eager student, and finally, gave his life to God and accepted Jesus as his Savior. They knelt in prayer, and after a big bear hug, Brady quietly left the chapel and headed toward the front door. As he passed the front office, he hesitated and poked his head through the door.

The lady behind the desk looked up and asked. "May I help you."

"My name is Brady Denney, and I just spent several weeks with one of the orphans, John, and I was wondering if you could give me any information about him and his background?"

"We aren't allowed to give out that kind of information, sorry!"

"Well, could you at least tell me what part of the country he is from."

"All I can tell you is that he is from somewhere out west, maybe Oregon or Idaho."

"Thank you, that is most helpful. Have a good evening!"

As he headed for his car, his senses quickened, and the picture began to clear. While he talked with John, he couldn't help but notice that he looked a lot like his brother, Casey. He had dismissed that thought, but with the information provided by the lady in the front office, the question became significant—could John be Casey's son? He vowed to take a closer look the next time they met.

"Hello, John, was your week okay?"

"Yes, it was better than okay. I feel really good about my decision to follow Christ."

"I'm so glad to hear that. Say, I have something I need to talk to you about, and it may come as somewhat of a surprise. But I think you can handle it."

"Okay, I'm always open to surprises."

"Well, I may as well just come right out and say it. You look just like my brother!"

"Your brother? How is that possible? What do you mean, brother? How could I look like him?"

"It's a long story, but the short version is, my brother, Casey Denney, spent the last seventeen years in prison in Idaho. He was convicted of fathering a child without a legal birth permit. His wife disappeared and was never found, so it was assumed that she died during the birth. That was never really proven, but there was enough evidence to also convict him of negligent criminal homicide. He finished his sentence this year, but no one knows for sure where he is. I checked with the orphanage office, and they think you were born somewhere in the Northwest, so it all may fit together, especially with you looking a lot like Casey."

"Wow, I really don't know what to say. I had dreamed of someday finding my parents, but had pretty much given up on the idea. I guess I really don't know what to do!"

"I certainly could leave the orphanage any time I wanted. I was just hanging around here because I didn't have any other place to go. It's hard to give up three meals a day and a warm place to sleep, and they don't seem to mind me hanging around. Besides, I don't have a lot of money and no prospect of a job on the outside."

"Well, you think, and we can talk some more next week."

"Fine, I look forward to it."

"Good, you think about it, and I'll see what I can do if you think you might want to try to find Casey."

A week later, Brady found John in his room. "Brady, I have been thinking about it, and I want to go to Idaho and see if I can find my father!"

"You do? Well, I have been thinking about it also and have some suggestions. I first thought that you might try to catch rides with truckers heading that way but decided against it—too risky and too uncertain. Instead, I am going to buy you a bus ticket to Nashville. Pete Jefferson and/or his wife Sheila will meet you and take it from there. They have agreed to help you figure out a way to get you to Idaho. How does that sound?"

"Great, sounds like a plan. Thank you so much. This means a lot to me. I still can't believe that I may have a family."

"Good, I'll meet you in the morning about 9:30. The bus leaves at 11:00. Do you have something to pack your things in?"

"Not really."
"I'll bring a backpack you can use. See you then."
"I'll be here and ready. See you then! Bye!"

Chapter 35
The Journey

*"For this God is our God for ever and ever;
He will be our guide even to the end" (Ps. 48:14, NIV).*

Brady and John arrived at the bus station just in time to buy John's ticket, have a word of prayer together, and John to board the bus. It was a beautiful, sunny early fall morning with not a cloud in the sky. The bus headed out of town and soon merged on to Interstate Highway 24. John had grabbed a window seat near the middle of the bus that provided him a good view of the Tennessee countryside. They soon left the heavy stop-and-go traffic, and the bus settled into a steady pace. John tilted the back of the seat into a comfortable position, and he soon dozed off. His rest was broken by the bus decelerating as it began a climb up the plateau, so he decided to take in the sights out of the bus window. Fall colors were at their peak, and he marveled at the red, yellow, orange blend that was displayed as they traveled through the hills. The wonder of God's creation was awesome, and he quietly thanked Jesus for sending Brady to him and providing him a way to have this experience and the chance to be united with a family—he hoped his family. Tears of joy welled up in his eyes as he imagined what it would be like!

John stepped off the bus and was greeted by a well-dressed middle-aged couple. The woman was the first to speak. "John? I'm Sheila

Jefferson, and this is my husband, Pete. Did Brady tell you we would meet you?"

"Yes!"

"Well, we are glad you are here, and we look forward to having you in our home for a few days while we figure out how we can help you. Brady said you wanted to try and find your father in Idaho."

"I'm not sure he is in Idaho, but that is where I would like to start. It is really kind of you to offer to help. I really appreciate it!"

"No problem, we are glad to do whatever we can. Brady and his family have been good friends for a long time, and we are happy to do what we can for them. Now, do you have any luggage?"

"No, ma'am, all I have is in this backpack Brady gave me."

"That's fine, then, let's head for the car and get you settled."

After a thirty-minute drive, they pulled into a long, curving driveway in front of a big, beautiful two-story house with immaculate landscaping and a big, wide double-door front entry. John had never seen anything like it, and as he exited the car, he stared in awe. He was shaken out of his trance by Pete. "John, John, is something wrong? Come on, let's go in and get you settled."

John followed Pete through the wide front door and into a large entry that opened to a spacious living room with huge picture windows that provided a view of a beautiful harbor and rows of boats at anchor. John had little time to enjoy the view as Pete motioned for him to follow up a curving staircase to the upper floor where he was guided to a well-decorated bedroom. "Here is where you can sleep. There is a private bathroom to the left and an empty closet to your right. Make yourself at home. I think Sheila is preparing us some supper. Freshen up, and come on down when you are ready."

Pete returned to the main floor and joined Sheila in the kitchen. "John seems like a good kid. How do you feel? Should we help him get to Idaho. I know you have been thinking about how ever since Brady called, and so have I. The issue is how do we do it? I would even drive him there, but I just can't take the time now. What are you thinking we should do?"

"First, I think we should let him stay with us for a few days, let me get him some new clothes and pray about what we should do then. There is no big hurry on our part, but I'm sure he is anxious to get going. We also need to spend some time praying about it and let God show us the way!"

She turned to set the food on the table, and John appeared. "Just take a seat anywhere around the table. Sheila was just finishing; hope you like haystacks!"

With the meal finished, Pete suggested that they move to the living room where it would be more comfortable. Sheila soon joined them, and without sitting down, offered a suggestion. "It's still early. I suggest we go to the mall and get John some new clothes. What do you think?"

Pete thought it was a good idea. John protested, claiming that he really did not need anything else. Sheila would not take no for an answer, so they headed for the car with John halfheartedly still protesting. The shopping took a few hours, and when they returned, John excused himself and headed for his room. Pete also headed for their bedroom, but Sheila remained behind to wash John's new clothes. It took some time to wash and dry the new clothes, so she quietly dropped them by John's room. He was fast asleep, but before leaving, she paused a minute to offer a short prayer in silence for John and his quest.

The next morning Pete and Sheila were sitting at the kitchen table, and after completing their morning devotional, Sheila suggested, "Pete, it's getting late, and I am about to fix breakfast. Would you go up and see how John is doing?"

"Okay, I can do that!"

When he returned, he had a worried look on his face.

"Pete, what's the matter? Where's John?"

"He's not in his room, and all his belongings, including the new clothes, are gone."

"What? How can that be?"

"He must have slipped out during the night."

"Well, you go get in the car and find him. We can't have that boy wandering around Nashville alone. Who knows what could happen to him?"

"Okay, I'll go see if I can find him. Should I call the police?"

"No, let's wait until you see if you can find him. I would check the bus depot and the interstate nearest here. Get going!!"

Pete returned a couple of hours later with no news of where John might be. Sheila met him at the door. "Nothing?"

"Nothing. I searched everywhere I thought he might be. I think I will call the State Highway Patrol."

Sheila handed him a piece of paper. "Before you make that call, I think you need to read this. I found it in his room after you left."

Pete read the note. "Why, that ungrateful little brat. How could he do this to us after we offered to help?"

"Now, Pete, be calm and think about it. He says he appreciated everything we did and just didn't want to impose on us anymore. He wants to make it on his own, and we have to respect that wish."

"I guess you are right. I just hope he makes it without any trouble!"

"He will. He has faith in God, and all we can do now is pray to God that He will protect him and give him strength."

John had walked until the sun was just coming up and spotted up ahead what he was looking for—a Pilot Truck Stop that he had noticed on the drive to the Jeffersons' house the day before. He hung around the truck pumps until he spotted what he was looking for. He was pretty sure the truck was an owner-operator rig. The driver was a rather stout middle-aged man, and he spotted a cross hanging from the center of the front windshield. He stayed a safe distance behind as he followed the driver into the building. He hung back as the driver paid the cashier and stopped at one of the displays to look for some snack food. John cautiously approached him. "Excuse me, sir, may I have a word with you?"

The driver looked at John with questioning but kind eyes. "What can I do for you, son? If you are looking for a handout, the answer is no!"

"I'm not looking for a handout, but I need to ask a favor."

"Okay, how can I help?"

John explained as briefly as he could about his need for a ride to Idaho and his desire to find his family.

The driver remained silent as he digested what he had been told. Normally he made it a hard and fast rule to never let anyone ride with him. He couldn't take the risk. But something in his head was impressing him to make an exception with this kid, and before he had time to think about it, he blurted out, "Okay, you can ride with me as far as Albuquerque. But you do what I say, and no funny business or I'll dump you on the side of the interstate and never look back."

"Oh, thank you, sir. I'll be no trouble, and I'll help you in any way I can."

"Fine! Have you had breakfast?"

"No. sir, but that's okay. I can wait."

"Nonsense, let's go get something to eat so we don't have to make a stop for a while. I said I wouldn't give you a handout, but I'll treat. You save your money; you may need it later. Now that I think about it, I feel

God opened the door for you, and I am supposed to make sure you get on down the road. By the way, my name is Robert, Robert Jones."

"I'm John, just John!"

After a typical truck stop breakfast, the two headed for Robert's rig and climbed on board. Soon they were heading west down Interstate 40 toward Memphis. Both were quiet for several miles. Finally, Robert broke the ice. "John, tell me a little more about yourself and what your life has been like."

John filled Robert in on his life at the orphanage and his time with Brady, including the revelation that he may have a family somewhere out west. He finished the story with another expression of his appreciation that Robert was willing to help him. They fell into another period of silence as Robert concentrated on keeping the rig on the road and staying clear of the darting and swerving four-wheelers. After a few more miles, he reached for the XM radio controls, and the voice of an International News anchor filled the cab.

"We have breaking news just in. The World Center for Disease Control (WCDC) has just released an announcement that there has been an outbreak in Western Europe. People are being infected with some sort of foul and loathsome sores. The WCDC sent a team of experts to determine the cause, and they reported that the infection seems to have affected a random sample of the population with no apparent common link in exposure, cleanliness, lifestyle, or diet. We expect to hear more from the WCDC later in our broadcast. Now for a commercial break!"

Robert and John remained silent for some time lost in their own thoughts about what they had just heard. They rode in silence until Robert pulled off the interstate and rolled into a truck stop near Galloway, Arkansas, just west of Little Rock. "Time to stretch our legs, make a pit stop, and grab a little food to keep us going. We are halfway to our final stop today near Oklahoma City. Take your time, but plan to be back in the truck in about twenty minutes."

John acknowledged the instructions and headed inside, looking for a restroom. He was back at the truck in fifteen minutes and found Robert waiting in the cab. "Ready to hit the road again?"

John took his seat on the passenger side. "Sure, let's do it."

As they got back on the interstate, Robert turned on the International News station.

"This just in regarding the earlier WCDC report. They have interviewed several people from both the infected group and the unaffected group. The

infected group has no idea where they got the disease. The majority of the unaffected group, however, are pointing to the Bible for the answer, specifically Revelation 16:1–2. The WCDC has dismissed their claim as preposterous and is continuing to gather information and samples for analysis. Yes, this just in. The infection has now spread to areas in Asia, Africa, South America, and some cases have been reported even here in North America. The WCDC suggests that you consult your family doctor immediately and report any sign of the infection to your local authorities."

Robert switched off the radio. "John, I have a Bible in the glovebox. Get it out and have a look at Revelation 16. Let's see what it says.

John retrieved the Bible and turned to Revelation 16. "Then I heard a loud voice from the temple saying to the seven angels, 'Go, pour out the seven bowls of God's wrath on the earth.' Verse 2, The first angel went out and poured out his bowl on the land, and ugly, festering sores broke out on the people who had the mark of the beast and worshiped its image."

John quickly glanced on down the chapter and saw that each one of the angels poured out their bowls, and there were other disasters and plagues that affected the earth. "Robert, do you suppose this is the beginning of the end right before Jesus comes back again?"

"It very well could be. I just hope I don't have the mark of the beast, whatever that is."

"I remember in one of our studies of the Bible, Brady mentioned the mark of the beast and told me that if I believed in Jesus and obeyed His laws, specifically the Ten Commandments, and

> *"I just hope I don't have the mark of the beast, whatever that is."*

especially the fourth commandment, I would never have the mark of the beast."

"Good to know. Well, let's get this rig down the road."

John put the Bible back in the glovebox, laid his head back in the seat and drifted off with visions still of what he had just read in the Bible.

The miles flew by. "John, wake up, we are in Oklahoma City. I'll fill up the fuel tanks and meet you in the restaurant. I'll also arrange for us to get a shower to shake off the traveling blues."

After a filling meal and shower, they returned to the truck. Robert crawled into the sleeper cab bunk. "John, sorry, buddy, but you will have to crash in the seat. I need all the rest I can get for the next leg. We should make Albuquerque by evening tomorrow. That is where I will have to leave you, but I will check with some of my driver friends to see if I can get you a ride from Albuquerque to Laramie and on into Salt Lake City. You will probably have to find something else to get you on to Idaho."

Robert was true to his word, and after two more full days of riding with trucker friends of Robert, John was happy to see that they were pulling into a truck stop in Salt Lake City. The driver insisted that they have prayer before they parted. He and John had spent many hours on the road, sharing experiences about how God had touched their lives, and the driver wished for John to have a safe and successful quest for his family. John thanked the driver for his kindness and also wished him well and God's blessing, then headed into the building.

He approached the clerk behind the cashier's counter. "Excuse me, but do you know if there is a Seventh-day Adventist Church near here?"

"Let me think. I seem to recall that there is one up on Foothill. I think if you go east on 2100 South, you will run right into it."

After a two-hour walk along 2100 South and across Foothill, John entered the open front door of the Wasatch Hills Seventh-day Adventist Church. He approached the three people in the lobby, two men and a woman, having a conversation. "Excuse me, is the pastor here? I'd like to speak to him."

One of the men offered his hand. "Hello, my name is Gordon, this is my wife Clarice, and pointing to the other man, this is our friend Steve. The pastor is not here. How can we help you?"

After introducing himself, John got to the point and related his experiences over the last few days and his desire to get to Twin Falls to search for his father.

Clarice was the first to respond. "My, you poor man, you must be exhausted and hungry. It's getting late. Please come home with us, and you can get some food and rest awhile. Then we can figure out how we can help you, okay?"

"Sure, I am a little tired, and a meal would be great, but I don't want to impose."

"You're not imposing; we are happy to help."

Seeing that he was not in the loop, Steve excused himself and headed for the door. "I'm heading home. We can talk later. Let me know if I can be of help."

Gordon pointed toward the door. "Clarice, you and John head for the car. I'll lock up and be with you in a minute."

After a hot shower, John joined Gordon and Clarice for a delicious meal that sure beat all that truck stop food that he had been eating the last three days. They then spent the next three hours talking about the infection that John had heard about on the satellite radio. Clarice and Gordon agreed that it could be the first of the plagues that would occur right before the second coming of Christ. Clarice then mentioned that she had a call that afternoon from a friend that had been watching the international news. The commentator said there were multiple reports of the oceans of the world turning red and dead fish and sea mammals washing up on beaches by the thousands. She posed the question, "Isn't that supposed to be the second plague?"

Her husband nodded in agreement. "Honey, you're so right. Let's look it up. John, I think you said Brady gave you a Bible. Want to look it up? I think it's in Revelation 16:3."

John read. *"The second angel poured out his bowl on the sea, and it turned into blood like that of a dead person, and every living thing in the sea died."*

"That's scary and a bit sobering. I hope I have enough time to find my father before any more plagues happen! I'm a bit tired, and if you don't mind, I'd like to get some sleep. I can crash on the couch if that's okay?"

"Of course not! We have an extra bed with some nice comfortable sheets that will fit you just fine. Come on. I'll show you where."

Soon John was in a very comfortable bed and fast asleep. The next morning, well-rested and anxious to continue on his journey, he joined the couple in the kitchen.

"Sit down and have some breakfast."

John took the seat across the table. "John, I made some calls last night after you went to bed, and the church is going to buy you a bus ticket to Twin Falls. It leaves in a couple of hours, so finish your breakfast, get ready, and we'll take you to the bus station and get you on your way. Is that okay with you?"

"You bet! That would be great. I can't thank you enough for your kindness and help. I hope that someday I will be able to repay you."

"Don't worry about repaying us, just help someone else if you get the chance."

Two hours later, John was on the bus to Twin Falls.

Chapter 36
The Final Quest

"But seek first his kingdom and his righteousness, and all these things will be given to you as well" (Matt. 6:33, NIV).

After four hours of a boring ride, the Greyhound bus arrived at the station in Twin Falls, Idaho. John gathered his backpack and entered the bus terminal to ask for directions to the county sheriff's office. After a forty-five-minute walk, he entered the sheriff's office and approached the receptionist's desk.

"How may we help you?"

"My name is John. I'd like to speak to the sheriff!"

"May I tell him what it is about?"

"I'm looking for a missing person."

"Okay, just a moment." The receptionist pushed a button on the intercom. "Sheriff, there is a young man here that says he is looking for a missing person."

John could not hear the reply, but in a few minutes, a man approached John with an outstretched hand. "Hi, I'm Sheriff Harry Mason. Come on in my office, and I'll see if we can help."

John followed the sheriff into his office and took one of the chairs in front of the desk. Harry took his seat behind the desk. "I understand you are looking for a missing person. Who might that person be?"

"Casey Denney."

Harry flashed a look of surprise. "Casey Denney! What is your connection to Casey Denney, and why do you say he is missing?"

Without hesitation, John responded. "I have reason to believe that I may be his son, and since I have no idea where he is, to me, he is missing, and I am trying to find him."

"What makes you think you might be his son?"

"His brother, Brady, convinced me that I might be. I have to find him and see if he is my father."

"You do know that he just recently was released from prison after serving a seventeen-year sentence for fathering a child without the proper birth permit." Harry withheld the part of the sentence for criminal negligent homicide.

"No, I didn't know that. But I don't think that makes a difference. I would still like to find him. Can you help?"

"I think I can; let me make a phone call. You can go back to the reception area and have a seat. I'll give it a try."

John returned to the reception area, and in a few minutes, Harry emerged from his office with a smile on his face. "John, I think we can help. I contacted the former sheriff, Darrin Scott, and he will be here shortly to pick you up. We think we know where we can start the search. Just relax. Can we get you anything—something to eat or drink?"

"No, thanks. I'm fine."

A half-hour passed, and a tall, graying man appeared through the front door, hesitated, and turned toward John. "You must be John. I'm Darrin Scott. I used to be sheriff, but I'm retired. I understand you are searching for Casey Denney. Well, I have a good idea where he might be. Come with me. We'll go to my home, you can spend the night, and in the morning, we will start the search. Sound good?"

"Sure, sounds good. Thanks. I appreciate it."

After a good meal prepared by Darrin's wife, Sherri, a good night's sleep, and a hearty breakfast, John and Darrin headed north out of Twin Falls in Darrin's four-wheel-drive pickup. They passed through miles of sagebrush desert sprinkled with fields of green that soon gave way to rolling hills.

"John, can I ask you a personal question?"

"Sure, what would you like to know?"

"Are you a Christian?"

"It depends what you mean by a Christian. I believe that Jesus or Christ, whatever you want to call him, was the Son of God and that He died on a cross so that I might have eternal life if I so choose. When I was with Brady, we did enough study of the Bible to convince me of that. But, if you mean am I a member of a specific Christian church, I am not a member of any church. I just believe in Christ, have chosen to give my life to Him, and follow wherever He leads me and have asked Him to guide me and give me the strength to do whatever He wants me to do. Does that answer your question?"

"Very much so. I'm glad to hear that you are a Christian. What do you think about the second coming of Jesus?"

"Funny, you should ask. In my travels to Idaho, I met two people who were convinced that we are in the last days of earth's history and that there have been at least two signs that verify that fact."

"What signs?"

"One, an infection that seems to affect only those that don't serve God and keep His commandments and two, an unexplained change in color of the world's oceans to red."

"I have heard reports of those events and believe they are the first two of the seven last plagues that God is pouring out on the earth right before Jesus returns. It's sobering, isn't it."

"I'm not worried about those plagues. I believe that God will protect me if I just trust him. I just hope I can find my dad before Jesus returns."

The rolling hills gave way to steep pine and aspen-covered slopes climbing from the banks of the South Fork of the Boise River. Darrin drove along the bank of the river for several miles and finally came to the end of the road where he parked the pickup. They got out of the pickup and walked to the bank of the river. Darrin pointed to the other bank of the river.

"See that stream on the other side, emptying into the river. That leads to Heart Lake. I think we may find your father there."

John followed Darrin as he crossed the river on the exposed rocks and began the climb up the trail. They soon arrived at what appeared to be a makeshift campsite, and as they approached, a bearded man appeared from behind a tree.

In spite of the beard, Darrin immediately recognized the man. "Casey, do you remember me?"

"Yes, you're the Twin Falls County Sheriff."

"Not anymore, I retired, but that is not important. What is important is I have brought someone you should meet! Casey, meet John. John thinks you are his father."

Casey had not really paid much attention to the young man who had invaded his privacy, but a bit startled, he turned his full attention from Darrin to John. "And what makes you think I am your father?"

Not to be intimidated, John moved closer to Casey. "Your brother Brady thinks I look a lot like you!"

Casey moved closer to John and looked closely into his eyes. "Yes, there is a resemblance, but there is only one way to tell for sure. Take off your shirt!"

John hesitated, looked at Casey, and then at Darrin and back to Casey. "I don't understand."

"You will if you just take off your shirt. Darrin, move in closer, you can be my witness. And John, turn around."

John turned around and removed his shirt. "Look, Darrin, there it is, a birthmark in the shape of a cross, right there in the small of his back. My son, John, had that birthmark! Yes, John, you are my son!"

Casey embraced John, and they both began to shed tears of joy.

Darrin stood watching the father and son begin a bond that was long overdue and half muttered to himself. "Well, I guess my job here is finished, and I'll be going. I can make it home before dark. If you need anything, get word to me. Probably not! Goodbye, and be safe. What am I saying? Casey knows how to survive up here, and he will take care of John. I'm happy for the two of you. So long." Darrin headed down the trail leaving the father and son to bond and be alone.

Chapter 37
Deliverance

*"From the L*ORD *comes deliverance" (Ps. 3:8, NIV).*

John and Casey spent the next two days getting better acquainted. Casey shared the stories of his life from as early as he could remember up to the present. John even got him to open up about his time in prison, which seemed to be an especially painful time and experience. Casey also managed to get John to share his experiences in the orphanage, which also to John, were troubling and painful. They spent several times in earnest prayer, not only thanking God for reuniting them but giving them strength to survive whatever was in their future.

On the third day, John finally had the courage to ask Casey about his mother. "Dad, I have been reluctant to bring this up, but do you know where my mother is?"

"Yes, John, I know where your mother is." Casey pointed down the trail. "We need to take a walk. I want to show you something."

John followed Casey down the trail, across the river, and along the road, retracing the path that Casey and Taylor had followed that fateful year John was born. At the steps of the cabin, Casey told John the story of his birth, the terrible death of his mother, and the events that eventually led to his arrest and imprisonment.

"Dad, thank you for telling me. I know it must have been hard to relive that awful time, but it has helped me understand a little about who and why I am. I wish I could have known her—maybe when we get to heaven. Do you think she is in heaven?"

"No, John, she is not in heaven. She is in a grave near Heart Lake, being watched over by an angel, and someday, when Jesus comes again, she will be resurrected, and then she will be in heaven." Tears welled up in his eyes. "I so look forward to that day."

"Dad, I have one other question. Why did I end up in an orphanage? Why didn't someone in the family take me?"

"John, they tried, but the government would not allow it. Mom and Dad tried hard and hired high-powered lawyers to try to keep you, but the government wouldn't budge. I was not a part of that fight, but as I understand it, under the law, children that are born without the proper permit are taken away and cannot stay with any member of their family. The government was so secretive that the family lost all track of where you were. I guess, theoretically, they could, even now, come and get you and take you away from me. I doubt that will happen. I'm sure they have much bigger problems. It must have been God's guidance that Brady found you. That answer your question?"

"Yes, I understand!"

"Good. But it's time to head back to camp. We need to be there before the sun goes down."

They retraced their steps along the river, back to the crossing, and started to step on the exposed rocks, but hesitated. "John, look at the water!"

John stared down at the cascading water and exclaimed, "It's red like blood!"

"Right, it's red. That can mean only one thing. It's the third plague of Revelation 16. Let's hurry back to camp. I hope the stream hasn't been changed; otherwise, we won't have any water to drink."

Much to their relief, when they returned to camp, the stream was still clear, and Casey quickly filled all of their water containers just in case.

The next morning after they arose, they noticed that the sun seemed to be particularly hot, and the temperature continued to climb to an almost unbearable level as the day progressed. They found some relief in the cool water of Heart Lake but finally had to retreat to the shade of a huge aspen tree to escape the intense heat. Casey wiped the sweat from his forehead and remarked, "I've never seen it this hot. I can't imagine how hot it must be down out of the mountains. I wouldn't want to be out in this very long. I'll be glad when the sun goes down."

The next day the sun was not so scorching, so they were able to follow the typical routine they had established, prayer and Bible study during the morning, a simple breakfast from all-natural plants, grains, and fruits, and an afternoon at Heart Lake swimming and fishing. John was beginning to feel relaxed, at home, and comfortable enjoying this new life with his father. Then the world came crashing down around them.

It was early in the morning the next day, and they were just starting their daily Bible study when there was a terrible roar followed by a rushing river of water that overflowed the stream and spread along the trail down the mountain. They quickly retreated to higher ground and made their way up to the lake. When they arrived, they were astonished to see that Heart Lake no longer existed. In its place was a jumbled pile of huge boulders, fallen trees, and jagged pieces of earth. The cliffs around the lake had crumbled and fallen into the crater that was once Heart Lake. In bewilderment, they returned to the campsite. It was destroyed. The rushing waters had pushed everything in its path down the trail. All they could do was stare blankly at the scene of utter devastation and wonder what they could do to survive.

Casey looked up as if he might find an answer from God. As he watched, there appeared a white cloud in the East about the size of a fist that grew rapidly bigger and bigger. He pointed it out to John, and for several minutes, they watched it as it continued to expand.

"Dad, do you think it might just be happening? I mean, Jesus's return. The second coming."

"Maybe, just maybe."

As Casey watched the expanding cloud, he felt something at his side. He turned to look and let out a cry of joy. There was Taylor by his side. She was radiant and more beautiful than he remembered. He rubbed his eyes. He must be seeing a ghost!

Sensing his bewilderment, Taylor broke the silence, "Yes, Casey, it's me, Taylor. I think it's time for us to go home. But who is this handsome young man with you?"

"Taylor, this young man is our son, John. He found me, and here we are, the three of us together, and now I know it's the second coming of Jesus."

"So, this is our son, John? Come here and give your mother a hug."

John eagerly obeyed, and the three of them stood tightly together with tightly-gripped hands as they watched the cloud get bigger and bigger."

"Taylor, you are so beautiful. I can't believe the time has really come. I'm ready to go home with you and John! But before we do, let's pray."

Gazing at the brightening sky, Casey prayed.

"*Lord, one more thing if You will. Please also save our family and friends that have also trusted You and have claimed Your saving grace.*"

The white cloud grew bigger, trumpets sounded, and songs of rejoicing filled the air. Then appeared a bright figure clothed in radiant white.

"Come, My brothers and sisters. It's time to go home."

For the Lord Himself will come down from heaven, with a loud command, with the voice of the archangel and with the trumpet call of God, and the dead in Christ will rise first. After that, we who are still alive and are left will be caught up together with them in the clouds to meet the Lord in the air. And so we will be with the Lord forever.

1 Thessalonians 4:16–17, NIV

TEACH Services, Inc.
P U B L I S H I N G

We invite you to view the complete
selection of titles we publish at:
www.TEACHServices.com

We encourage you to write us
with your thoughts about this,
or any other book we publish at:
info@TEACHServices.com

TEACH Services' titles may be purchased in
bulk quantities for educational, fund-raising,
business, or promotional use.
bulksales@TEACHServices.com

Finally, if you are interested in seeing
your own book in print, please contact us at:
publishing@TEACHServices.com
We are happy to review your manuscript at no charge.

www.ingramcontent.com/pod-product-compliance
Lightning Source LLC
Chambersburg PA
CBHW070555160426
43199CB00014B/2510